THE PIG BOOK

How Government Wastes Your Money

★ ★ ★ ★ ★ ★

BY

Citizens Against Government Waste

Thomas Dunne Books/St. Martin's Griffin
New York

THOMAS DUNNE BOOKS.
An imprint of St. Martin's Press.

www.stmartins.com

Library of Congress Cataloging-in-Publication Data Available Upon Request

ISBN 0-312-34357-4
EAN 978-0312-34357-6

First Edition: May 2005

10 9 8 7 6 5 4 3 2 1

For J. Peter Grace, Jack Anderson, and the millions of taxpayers who had to pay for these projects.

To advocate an efficient, sound, honest government is neither left-wing nor right-wing. It is just plain right.
—J. Peter Grace

CONTENTS

FOREWORD BY SEN. JOHN McCAIN

In January 1984, J. Peter Grace, the cofounder of Citizens Against Government Waste, wrote to then-President Ronald Reagan that eliminating waste and abuse in the federal government was necessary so that "our children and grandchildren would not inherit a situation that would be devastating to them and to the values of our economic and social system." Sadly, those words, written 21 years ago, still apply today.

While we have seen some improvements since 1984, we still have much work to do in order to eliminate the wasteful practices of our government. Our nation faces a projected deficit of nearly half a trillion dollars and we continue to spend and spend and spend. There is a misconception that Republicans and Democrats can't find any common ground. I have even lamented on how nasty and partisan Washington has become. Well, I stand corrected, because there is one thing which unites Republicans and Democrats: Fiscal irresponsibility, the one great unifier of late. And for that, we should all be ashamed.

From pork-barrel spending to expanding entitlements, both parties have proven who they represent and who they are working for, and it's not the American taxpayer. It seems as if Republicans and Democrats alike represent no one but the special interests. Whether it be catfish farmers in the South, blueberry farmers in the North, or big pharmaceutical companies with high-paid lobbyists in Washington—big-monied special interests have a stranglehold on our nation's Capitol.

We are at war, and throughout history wartime has been a time of sacrifice. At the beginning of the war I said it would be long and difficult, and would require a great deal of sacrifice on everyone's part. But about the only sacrifice taking place is that by the brave men and women fighting to defend and protect the liberties we hold so dear.

It is time for others to step up and sacrifice, starting with Congress's appetite for pork. In the last several years Congress has approved legislation containing billions and billions of dollars in unrequested and unauthorized pork-barrel projects, and a corporate tax bill chock full of billions of dollars in tax breaks for wealthy oil and gas companies and other special interests estimated to cost $180 billion. That is a far cry from true sacrifice.

In 1994, Republicans won control of both Houses of Congress. For one brief shining moment, we employed true fiscal restraint and eventually managed to balance the budget and even attain that which had seemed unattainable—a surplus! Now, at a time of national crisis, we have thrown caution to the wind and continue to spend and spend and spend. The perfect evidence of this is the number of Congressional earmarks found in the 13 annual appropriations bills. In 1994 there were 1,318 pork-barrel projects; in fiscal year 2005 there are an estimated 13,000 pork-barrel projects, an increase of 886 percent. Where are our priorities?

So who are we hurting by this outrageous spending? Peter Grace's words haunt us: We're hurting our children, our grandchildren, and who knows how many future generations of Americans. And for what? So that members of the House and the Senate can go home in an election year and brag about a peanut festival in Alabama or an indoor rain forest in Iowa. Or to keep the special interests happy. It is my greatest hope that someday Congress will consider the financial well-being of taxpayers when passing spending bills.

My friends at Citizens Against Government Waste are to be commended for their many years of good work. I believe that this book should be read by every citizen in America. What is being done by Citizens Against Government Waste, in my view, is of the greatest importance. I will continue to rely on their expertise as we work together to find ways to make our government more accountable to the American taxpayer.

INTRODUCTION

Given Congress's proclivity toward wasting tens of billions of dollars on pork-barrel projects every year, one would think the practice has been around since the inception of the Republic. That would be close, but not quite correct. Unfortunately, far too many members of Congress protect and defend pork-barrel spending with such passion that they practically consider it a constitutional right.

The appearance of Punxsutawney Phil, the world-famous groundhog, at a December 2004 press conference in Washington, D.C., is ample evidence of how far representatives and senators will go to justify their pet projects. The poor rodent was woken from his winter slumber to demonstrate the apparent necessity to spend $100,000 for the Punxsutawney Weather Discovery Center, inserted into the Consolidated Appropriations Act of 2005 by Rep. John Peterson (R-Pa). Phil did not look all that happy, and in fact urinated on the table during the event, expressing how taxpayers really feel about pork-barrel spending.

Citizens Against Government Waste (CAGW) wrote in its press release that "Phil seemed to be happy burrowing holes in the ground; but now he is burrowing holes in taxpayers' wallets. On the real Groundhog Day, instead of waking up and seeing his shadow, he will see 10 more years of deficits. Unfortunately, taxpayers will not be able to hibernate through the coming crisis in entitlement spending, sure to be made worse by Congress's addiction to pork spending."

Phil and Rep. Peterson were named by CAGW as the co-porkers of the month for December 2004, for "defending questionable priorities in a time of war, record deficits, and debt; circumventing the budget process; and grabbing $100,000 in federal funding for a pet project."

All of this would lead a reasonable taxpayer to conclude that you can't make up the stuff that Congress does with our tax dollars.

Pork-barrel spending is almost as old as the Republic, but the term "pork-barrel" itself is not quite that dated. Its non-political meaning has its origins in the U.S. colonial practice of handing out salt pork to slaves. After a long day in the fields, slaves would rush to the pork barrel for food.

Now, the term relates to members of Congress scurrying to the U.S. Treasury to grab tax dollars that will be doled out to their states and districts. The expression first began circulating in its political context around 1905, but the practice can be traced back as early as the Bonus Bill, legislation to build highways connecting the East and the South to the Western Frontier in 1817.

In 1988, President Reagan took a pile of appropriations bills stuffed with pork and dropped them on the floor during his State of the Union address. He promised to stop the waste, pushed for a line-item veto, and tried to restrain the growth of the federal government.

One of Reagan's most ambitious projects was the President's Private Sector Survey on Cost Control, which became better known as the Grace Commission after its chairman, industrialist J. Peter Grace. Reagan asked Grace, along with 161 senior business executives and 2,000 volunteers, to "work like a tireless bloodhound" to root out waste, mismanagement, and inefficiency in the federal government. One of the better-known Grace Commission discoveries was that the Department of Defense spent $436 for a hammer and $640 for a toilet seat. When asked about the latter expenditure, a Pentagon spokesperson said that then-Secretary Caspar Weinberger was sitting on the problem. After the Grace Commission finished its work, Grace joined with Pulitzer Prize-winning, nationally syndicated columnist Jack Anderson to form CAGW.

Over the last two decades, pork-barrel spending in particular has become more notorious in part due to the ugly truth about members of Congress: They waste tax dollars like drunken sailors on shore leave (which may be insulting to our fine men and women in uniform). In the most recent example of such excess, on December 10, 2004, President Bush signed into law the fiscal year 2005 Consolidated Appropriations Act (also called the omnibus spending bill), which funded nine of the 13 appropriations bills. These bills give Congress the legal authority to spend money from the U.S. Treasury. The omnibus bill was enacted more than two months after the beginning of fiscal year 2005 (October 1, 2004), and was loaded with special-interest projects added by members of Congress at the last minute.

The $388 billion bill included: $1.5 million for a demonstration project to transport naturally chilled water from Lake Ontario to Lake Onondaga; $500,000 for the Kincaid Soccer Park and Nordic Ski Center in Anchorage, Alaska; $100,000 for the

Tiger Woods Foundation; $80,000 for the San Diego Gay, Lesbian, Bisexual, and Transgender Community Center; $75,000 for the Paper Industry International Hall of Fame in Appleton, Wisconsin; and $25,000 for curriculum development for the study of mariachi music in the Clark County School District, Nevada. With typical inside-the-Beltway perspective, House Appropriations Committee Chairman Bill Young (R-Fla.) called the omnibus bill "lean and clean."

Unfortunately, neither the pork nor the chairman's nonchalance was an anomaly. Every year since 1991, CAGW has published the annual *Congressional Pig Book* to expose the pork-barrel antics of Congress in the 13 appropriations bills. There have been 52,461 pork-barrel projects worth $185 billion. While the term "pork" has been used for a wide range of government waste and is sometimes interchanged with "earmarks" (which have a much broader connotation), CAGW established a set of criteria, in conjunction with the Congressional Porkbusters Coalition, to determine whether a project qualifies as pork-barrel spending.

In CAGW's view, the term "pork barrel" refers to any project that has not gone through the proper process to receive funding. In order to be included in the *Congressional Pig Book*, a project must meet one of the following seven criteria:

🐷 requested by only one chamber of Congress;
🐷 not specifically authorized;
🐷 not competitively awarded;
🐷 not requested by the President;
🐷 greatly exceeded the President's budget request or the previous year's funding;

🐖 not the subject of congressional hearings; or

🐖 served only a local or special interest.

These criteria are important because Congress established specific rules through which projects must pass in order to receive funding. In essence, these pork-barrel projects break Congress's own rules, showing continued disrespect for our tax dollars.

The Pig Book: How Government Wastes Your Money will take readers down memory lane with the most egregious examples of pork-barrel spending since 1991. So hold on to your wallets and keep your doctor's phone number handy, as CAGW is not responsible for any adverse physical reaction, including a stroke or heart attack, when you read about what Congress has been doing with *your* money.

THE
PIG BOOK

Agriculture:
Pork on the Range

American agriculture conjures up images of amber waves of grain and purple mountain majesties, with farmers waking at dawn to milk the cows and feed the pigs and chickens. For the members of the U.S. Congress, the Agriculture Appropriations Act is the prime opportunity to send pork back to their district or state.

Millions of dollars in agriculture research are funded through this appropriation. In fiscal year 2004, $111 million was appropriated for special research grants even though the U.S. Department of Agriculture (USDA) only requested $3 million. At first glance, this may seem sensible, but the reality is that most of the research benefits particular commodities or states. The USDA has repeatedly warned Congress not to fund any state- or commodity-specific research, citing that it is not the federal government's responsibility.

$102 Million for Screwworm Research

There is nothing like getting "screwed" by the government. The initial $33.4 million dumped into this particular research program in 1991 created quite a buzz on Capitol Hill. Critics sat bewildered as members of Congress appropriated the loot for screwworm research. Apparently someone forgot to tell them that this flesh-eating fly was eradicated in the 1970s.

The little bugger was pushed south as far as Panama, but the USDA claims research is needed because beef in Central America may still carry the parasite. No word on why Central America can't pay for its bug problem. But we should "bug out" of this debate.

$9.9 Million for the Rural Policies Research Institute

The Rural Policies Institute (Arkansas, Iowa, Missouri, and Nebraska) has been a cash cow since 1992, when the appropriations committees dumped $525,000 into the research. The institute "conducts policy-relevant research and facilitates public dialogue to assist policymakers in understanding the rural impacts of public policies and programs." Hint: One of the bad policies is subsidies.

$7.4 Million for Peanut-related Research

Whether chowing down on Kung Pao chicken or your favorite candy bar, peanuts are a staple of American cuisine. Peanut research has also become a staple of appropriators' cuisine. Included in the $7.4 million total: $1.54 million for the National Center for Peanut Competitiveness at the University of Georgia in Athens, Georgia; $1.3 million for peanut research in the state of House Agriculture Appropriations Subcommittee Member Jack Kingston (R-Ga.); and $47,000 for peanut breeding.

The center is an absurd waste of money because the federal peanut program restricts the acreage for growing peanuts, preventing any marketplace competition. There was more nutty spending in 2001: The Senate appropriated $500,000 for peanut allergy reduction research in Alabama. In November 1998, Senate appropriator Richard Shelby (R-Ala.) released a statement opposing federal involvement in peanut allergy concerns, calling it "overreaching" and precisely what makes Americans question the government's "common sense." But three years later, Sen. Shelby abandoned his own common sense by voting to earmark $500,000 for more peanut allergy research.

$1.7 Million for the Center for Rural Studies

Since 1992, the Center for Rural Studies in Vermont has received an annual gift from Congress, courtesy of Agriculture Committee Ranking Member and Senate appropriator Patrick

Leahy (D-Vt.). Just looking at the name of the research provides very little insight into its purpose. But, according to USDA testimony, funds in the past have been used for "analytical reports provided to a retail shopping mall to help it attract new businesses to fill vacant space. . . ." How about having the mall's owners pay for their own advertising?

$3.2 Million for Cranberry/Blueberry Research

New Jersey and Massachusetts have walked away with $3.2 million for cranberry/blueberry research. But that's a drop in the bucket. According to congressional testimony, "The researchers anticipate that significant solutions to the many interrelated pests and production problems will require an additional three to ten years especially to develop improved cultivars."

$15.6 Million for Swine Research

Since Congress is constantly "porking up" the budget, there may not be a more appropriate area of research, although there's no truth to the rumor that these projects are located under the U.S. Capitol. Swine research includes $3,442,000 in North Carolina and $539,000 in Minnesota. In 2002, Rep. John Boehner (R-Ohio) chastised his colleagues with jabs at such piggish funding:

Winning the War on Terrorism. Securing our homeland. Modernizing our military to ensure readiness and supremacy. Increasing the flexibility of states, local communities, and parents to provide a high-quality education for every child. And putting more money back into the wallets of hardworking, overtaxed American men and women. Are these good uses of federal funds? You bet. But how about cash for manure management research at the National Swine Research Center in Iowa? Or a government grant for Hawaiian sea turtles? Or taxpayer dollars used to fund a tattoo removal program in San Luis Obispo, California? The list goes on and on. Are these good uses of federal funds? Sadly, it depends on who you ask. You see, when it comes to "pork projects" like these, too many congressional Democrats and Republicans are equal opportunity squealers. And even in the midst of a war, a period of economic uncertainty, and a temporary return of budget deficits, some of my colleagues contribute to an already bloated federal bureaucracy by quietly sliding 'earmarked' pet projects into federal appropriations bills each year. And the current fiscal year is no exception.

$2.7 Million for Lowbush Blueberry Research

Appropriators find their thrills on Blueberry Hill. This research is being conducted at the University of Maine, home state of Republican Senators Susan Collins and Olympia Snowe. Lowbush blueberries are not planted, but are common forest groundcover plants. About 60,000 acres of lowbush blueberry are managed in Maine, which produces 99 percent of all the blueberries hitting the U.S. market. So why doesn't Maine foot the bill, then?

It's because blueberries intrigue Congress. In 2002, Congress dished out $10 million of taxpayers' money for blueberry purchases; that same year, Senators Collins and Snowe teamed up with the Wild Blueberry Commission of Maine and pushed USDA officials to buy the blue fruit. According to a 2002 *Wall Street Journal* article, the $10 million would buy about 12 million pounds of wild blueberries—between 16 and 17 percent of the entire industry crop of 70 million to 75 million pounds of berries in an average year.

"Why all the fuss for a fruit that sells at a premium and that grows naturally throughout New England, New York and elsewhere?" asked the *Journal*. "Politicians, of course," who "love to harvest the federal government's bounty for home-state farmers. The wild-blueberry industry is small and therefore easy to enrich. The industry is also almost entirely located in Maine—by one estimate, 99 percent of commercially picked wild blueberries come from that state. What's more, blueberries have been a staple of the rural economy for decades—if not centuries—and are now part of the state's culture. Supporting such an industry is an easy political decision. Oppose it and you'll be opposing the local farm stand's wild-blueberry pies and hot, fresh muffins."

$64.4 Million for Shrimp Aquaculture Research in Arizona, Hawaii, Louisiana, Massachusetts, Mississippi, South Carolina, and Texas

This little creature sure proposes big problems for American taxpayers. An internal USDA audit obtained by CAGW details abuse by one of the grant recipients, the Oceanic Institute (OI) of Hawaii. In addition to USDA, OI was audited by the Department of Commerce and the Agency for International Development. According to the USDA inspector general, OI "did not comply with Federal regulations or with the terms of the grant agreements. OI used grant funds for purposes that were not specified in its grant budgets and that were not approved by ARS (Agricultural Research Service) or CSREES (Cooperative State Research, Education, and Extension Service). It also made unallowable procurements with related parties and did not always perform required cost analyses, document the bases for contractor selection, or justify the lack of competition when procuring goods and services."

Even so, that hasn't stopped Congress from appropriating funds to the shrimp industry since 1985. This research is currently being undertaken in Arizona, Hawaii, Massachusetts, Mississippi, Louisiana, South Carolina, and Texas. In case legislators happened to forget their geography lessons: Arizona is a landlocked state. This little detail didn't escape Sen. John McCain (R-Ariz.), who in 2001 stated that "I always am intrigued by the vision of little shrimp flopping around out in the desert."

$5.4 Million for the Food Marketing Policy Center

The Food Marketing Policy Center (FMPC) at the University of Connecticut (UConn) in Storrs, Connecticut, is located in the district of ex-farmer and UConn alumnus Sam Gejdenson (D-Conn.). While FMPC claims "the general intent is to provide information that can contribute to improved performance of the food production and marketing system," it may be more apparently dedicated to consuming our tax dollars. One of the center's projects has been researching the pricing and marketing of cereal—a task one would think could be determined by the cereal companies, families, and children at no cost to taxpayers.

$5.94 Million for the North Central Biotechnology Initiative

This project was established in 1995 to be a "competitive" grants program. It wasn't, so USDA proposed no funds for this project in fiscal year 1997, and USDA officials stated that, in keeping with the "Administration's policy of awarding research grants competitively, no further federal funding for this grant is requested." Apparently the House didn't get the memo, because it appropriated $1.94 million for the project in fiscal year 1997.

$23.2 Million for Human Nutrition Research

While a handful of research centers and universities conduct human nutrition research, the $473,000 study in Iowa sticks out. In 1997, some of that money was used to develop low-fat snack foods, such as "Soy-nog," a low-fat, low-cholesterol version of eggnog.

$9.3 Million for Floriculture Research

While funding for floriculture research in the state of Senate appropriator Daniel Inouye (D-Hawaii) was expected to be done by fiscal year 1996, it didn't stop the Senate's annual allotment for the research. USDA officials also specifically stated that this program should be funded by the state of Hawaii. Hawaii's response? Why bother when Uncle Sam is pollinating the state with tax dollars? This research is expected to help the $50 million cut flower and foliage industry in Hawaii.

$10.4 Million for the Viticulture Consortium

Physicians have stated that a glass of red wine is good for the heart. Drink up because reading about how much money has been appropriated for the wine industry may cause a coronary. According to USDA testimony, this research is designed to "help the viticulture [grape] and wine industries remain competitive in the United States and in the global market." The mission of the Viticulture Consortium, located in California and New York, is to:

- ⚜ Understand grape physiology and develop cultivation methods that lead to sustainable and economical production of grapes;
- ⚜ Determine the impact of grapevine cultivation practices on chemical traits that affect the quality of wines and other grape products produced in different geographical regions;
- ⚜ Improve the productivity of grapes and quality of grape products by selecting and breeding scion and rootstock varieties; and
- ⚜ Improve understanding of the biology of pests and diseases, and develop integrated crop management programs for specific grape production regions that are economically feasible, environmentally sound, and socially acceptable.

Wine sales in the U.S. grew 5 percent to a record 627 million gallons in 2003, with a retail value of $21.6 billion—a 2.3 percent increase over the previous year. California alone produced 417 million gallons, which accounted for a 67 percent share of the market, two of every three bottles sold in the U.S. Export figures jumped an estimated 17 percent over the previous year (about 95 percent of exported product came from California) to $643 million in winery revenues, and surged 29 percent by volume to 96 million gallons.

Who needs a drink?

$1.75 Million for Agricultural Diversification and Specialty Crops in Hawaii

Senate appropriator Daniel Inouye (D-Hawaii) has grabbed $1.75 million for agricultural diversification and specialty crops projects for his state. Along with their "lei project," researchers are also trying to obtain marketing orders for Maui onion growers—a stinky result for taxpayers.

$10.5 Million for the National Warmwater Aquaculture Center in Stoneville, Mississippi

Congress seems to have quite an appetite for fish farms. The National Warmwater Aquaculture Center received $3,308,000 between 1999 and 2001 to research catfish production. The aquaculture industry earned more than $500 million in 1997, whereas Congress spent $9.4 million that same year on various aquaculture research projects, including $370,000 on Chesapeake Bay aquaculture; $330,000 on aquaculture research in Louisiana; and $127,000 on multi-cropping strategies for aquaculture in Hawaii.

$7.25 Million for Grasshopper Research

Congress has appropriated $7.25 million for grasshopper research, including $75,000 in 1992 and 1993 for grasshopper biocontrol in North Dakota. But that doesn't compare with the $750,000 added by the Senate in 1999 for grasshopper research in the state of Senate Appropriations Committee Chairman Ted Stevens (R-Alaska). Doesn't a frozen grasshopper simply require crème de menthe, crème de cocoa, and vanilla ice cream?

$21.9 Million for the National Center for Cool and Cold Water Aquaculture in Leetown, West Virginia

Senate Appropriations Committee Ranking Member Robert C. Byrd (D-W.Va.) is making sure money flows regularly to the National Center for Cool and Cold Water Aquaculture in Leetown, West Virginia. According to USDA, the center consists of a tank/aquarium building of approximately 20,000 square feet and a laboratory/office complex of approximately 30,000 square feet. The center opened in 2001, employing five scientists and five support staff. At full capacity, 12 full-time scientists and 18 support personnel will work at the facility.

$650,000 for Alternative Salmon Products Research

Senate Appropriations Committee Chairman Ted Stevens (R-Alaska) has sold taxpayers up the river for this research. In

2002, Alaskan salmon fishers netted around $220 million in profits. According to the *Anchorage Daily News*, the waters of Valdez swelled with an estimated 22 million salmon in 2003, the largest amount ever recorded. With the overabundance of salmon, the city decided to entice tourists by giving a free salmon to anyone who visited Valdez during the summer tourist months. That makes the industry a lot more solvent than most taxpayers.

$728,000 for Vidalia Onion Research

Known for its sweet taste, the Vidalia onion is grown in only a handful of counties in Georgia. House Agriculture Appropriations Subcommittee Member Jack Kingston (R-Ga.) has been the biggest supporter for research of these onions. In the past, money has been used for "pungency testing" and is now supposed to go toward onion disease research. According to testimony by USDA officials, this research will solely benefit the state of Georgia and the Vidalia onion industry.

The Vidalia onion has become a sweet source of revenue for Georgia, and chopping this subsidy from the budget would certainly make some folks cry. According to the Vidalia Onion Committee, its industry pulls in an estimated $95 million annually for the state and accounts for 13 percent of Georgia's vegetable cash receipts. Similar onions are grown in other states, including Texas and Washington, but none of them get such a sweet subsidy.

$2.2 Million for Satsuma Orange Research

Members of Congress putting the squeeze on taxpayers is nothing new. While USDA has never requested funds for Satsuma orange research, it didn't matter. Senate appropriator Richard Shelby (R-Ala.) and House appropriators Robert Aderholdt (R-Ala.), Sonny Callahan (R-Ala.), and Robert Cramer (D-Ala.) freshly squeezed the money out of the taxpayers. The focus of this research is to determine new methods for Satsuma orange production, an important crop in Alabama, "under potentially unfavorable conditions." Its national significance remains dubious. The Satsuma is a nearly seedless orange and is a descendant of the Mandarin orange, once reserved for China's privileged class. Now it is reserved for the privileged porkers in Alabama.

$79 Million for Wood Utilization Research

Talk about sapping taxpayers for research! Get a load of this: Wood utilization research for Alaska, Idaho, Maine, Michigan, Minnesota, Mississippi, North Carolina, Oregon, Tennessee, Washington, and West Virginia cost taxpayers $6.1 million alone in fiscal year 2004. It's been funded since 1985, with no end—or purpose—in sight.

$538,000 for the National Wild Turkey Federation

The National Wild Turkey Federation (NWTF), located in Edge-field, South Carolina, is "a half million member grassroots, non-profit organization with members in 50 states, Canada, and 11 other foreign countries." With 500,000 members, this organization could raise $538,000 with just another $1.08 per member.

NWTF has a little something for everyone: numerous conservation projects, a Web page dedicated to turkey hunting tips and tactics, and a large list of the best outdoor gear for hunters. The group also collects turkey feathers to donate to the Zuni Nation of New Mexico for use in religious ceremonies, and it even shares some of the best turkey recipes from around the nation. Like all other organizations, NWTF includes information on how to donate to the group. Congress must have signed up to be an annual giver. Gobble, gobble.

Commerce, Justice, State, and the Judiciary: To Protect and Defend Congressional Pork

Americans are counting on the Departments of Commerce, Justice, and State to execute key objectives in the war on terror: to hold together diplomatic coalitions, monitor intelligence for future threats, guard borders, improve trade relations and economic conditions overseas, and bring terrorists to justice. Yet appropriators have continually diverted critically needed funds from the three departments to fund pet projects. While there is a wide range of pork-barrel projects, the lion's share happens to reside in Alaska and Hawaii.

$1 Million for the Alaska Beluga Whale Committee

Located in the state of Senate Appropriations Committee Chairman Ted Stevens (R-Alaska), the Alaska Beluga Whale Committee (ABWC) was founded in 1988. Composed of whale hunters and scientists, the committee works to "encourage con-

servation and informed management of beluga whales and to in-
volve Native subsistence hunters in the management of this important resource."

According to its Web site, federal funding has helped ABWC:

🐷 Adopt the Alaska Beluga Whale Management Plan;
🐷 Obtain harvest information;
🐷 Pay for representatives to attend meetings;
🐷 Conduct aerial surveys and genetic stock and contaminant
studies; and most importantly,
🐷 Produce some nice-looking newsletters.

It's no wonder the deficit is as big as a whale!

$44.6 Million for Alaskan Salmon

Sen. Stevens has secured $44.6 million for Alaskan salmon
restoration, conservation, and research projects since 1991.
One of the projects, "alternative salmon products" research,
has received $3,925,000 since fiscal year 1998, the same year
that Alaska's senator had become chairman of the Senate Appropriations Committee. The Alaska Science and Technology
Foundation has conducted "alternative salmon products" studies, and in a 1994 research project, a company was attempting
to "develop an innovative, marketable, convenient and tasty,
pink salmon product." Once the company had developed a
"skinless pink salmon fillets for a baked, frozen, microwaveable
entrée" it expected to "become a major producer of innovative

value-added salmon products in Alaska, with annual sales of $5 million in four years, growing to $15 million annually in seven to ten years. The primary benefit from this project will be a value-added product that will assist the commercial fishing industry."

Some of the "necessary" salmon conservation and enhancement initiatives include public education programs, studying a parasitic infection on chum salmon, and a project to prevent Pacific salmon from escaping from the state's streams. The last project must have been successful. A summer 2004 *Anchorage Daily News* article reported that in Valdez, Alaska, officials used salmon to bait tourists to come and visit their town. The 2003 pink salmon run totaled 22 million in Valdez, the largest run on record for the city.

$800,000 for the Alaska Native Harbor Seals Commission

Since 1999, the Alaska Native Harbor Seals Commission (ANHSC) has received $800,000 in pork (or should we say blubber), thanks to Senate Appropriations Committee Chairman Ted Stevens (R-Alaska). The commission's mission is to "ensure that harbor seals remain an essential cultural, spiritual, and nutritional element of [Alaska's] way of life." The ANHSC conducts data analyses, population monitoring, and biological sampling.

Although a harbor seal's diet varies, one of its favorite delicacies is salmon. Maybe Sen. Stevens is spending all that money on salmon just to save the seals. The food chain of life and the flow of pork seem to come together in Alaska, thanks to Sen. Stevens.

$10.9 Million for the Oceanic Institute in Hawaii

Senate Commerce, Justice, State, and the Judiciary Appropriations Subcommittee Member Daniel Inouye (D-Hawaii) has funneled $10.9 million for two programs of the Oceanic Institute (OI) in Hawaii: the Hawaiian Fisheries Development Project and the Hawaii Stock Management Plan. A 1995 audit by the USDA revealed that the OI misused the grant money it had received from the USDA. According to the USDA inspector general, OI "did not comply with Federal regulations or with terms of the grant agreements. OI used grant funds for purposes that were not specified in its grant budgets and that were not approved by ARS (Agriculture Research Service) or CSREES (Cooperative State Research, Education, and Extension Service). It also made unallowable procurements with related parties and did not always perform required cost analyses, document the bases for contractor selection, or justify the lack of competition when procuring goods and services." In flagrant dismissal of this report, Senator Inouye added $1,250,000 each year for OI in fiscal years 1996, 1997, and 1998.

The research conducted for the stock enhancement project is funded mainly by the National Marine Fisheries Service (NMFS) of the National Oceanic and Atmospheric Administration (NOAA). One of the goals of the project is "to apply aquaculture technology to the enhancement of depleted nearshore fish populations." Scientists involved in the program examine Pacific threadfin, called "moi" in Hawaii, to understand "how stock enhancement may affect the moi ecosystem, as well as genetic studies to determine the long-term effects of the released fish on multiple generations." From 1991 to 2004, Congress appropriated $4.9 million for the Hawaii Stock Management Plan.

NOAA also manages the Hawaiian Fisheries Development Project, which has reeled in $6 million since fiscal year 1994, thanks to Sen. Inouye. The project received funding via a directed, non-competitive grant, which circumvented federal grant procedure, causing NOAA to question "the Institute's financial condition and ability to administer grants, and the project's relationship to the NOAA mission." The House wasn't as diplomatic: "The House bill eliminates or reduces below current levels almost all programs located in the State of Hawaii."

The goal of the Hawaiian Fisheries Development Project is "to generate new information, technologies, and products to assist both fishery management and marine finfish aquaculture development in Hawaii and throughout the U.S. The approach is to compare and contrast the biological patterns of reproduction, growth, and development of different, economically significant warm-water fish species. As such, the [Fisheries Development] Project plays a pivotal role in warm-water aquaculture development in the United States and provides key input to U.S. marine fishery restoration initiatives." Typical of the government, Congress has appropriated funds for parallel projects, including the Warmwater Aquaculture Center in Stoneville, Mississippi (see Agriculture).

$60.5 Million for the East-West Center in Honolulu, Hawaii

The East-West Center (EWC), located in the state of Sen. Inouye, works to promote better relations and understanding between the U.S. and the nations of Asia and the Pacific through cooperative research, study, and training programs. Although there was a budget and Senate request for this project in fiscal year 1999, the House refused to give it any funds. The House Appropriations Committee pointed out that the center can solicit private contributions or compete for federal grants to support its activities, so it does not need a direct federal subsidy. On top of the $60.5 million in unrequested pork-barrel appropriations, the center has received approximately $200 million from the State Department in the last 10 years.

EWC funds various activities and workshops on topics such as community-based forestry and concerns about premarital sex, and holds a biannual international fair with music, dance, crafts, and games. The organization has generous corporate contributors. The McInerny Foundation matches alumni donations 1:1, up to $100 each. The Hawaii Pacific Rim Society supports projects and programs such as the "Huun-Huur-Tu: Throat Singers of Tuva" performance in February 2004, and the "Masks of Southeast Asia" exhibition and performance-demonstrations in July and September 2004. The society has also provided a "generous contribution" to the Ariyoshi Fund to provide financial assistance to East-West Center students. The Bank of Hawaii finances "AsiaPacific Breakfast Briefings," which are attended by Hawaiian business and community leaders and the center's members who contribute $100 or more.

$17.6 Million for the Dante B. Fascell North-South Center at the University of Miami, Florida

A longitudal answer to the East-West Center, the North-South Center (NSC) was created in 1984 and is run by the university in collaboration with the RAND Corporation. The center works to promote good relations among the U.S., Canada, Latin America, and the Caribbean. Research conducted at the center focuses on trade and economic policy, migration, democratic governance, security, corruption, the environment, and information technology.

NSC began receiving a direct subsidy from the federal government in 1991, but prior to that time it operated on private funding and competed for and received project-specific grants. The Senate continually added funds for the center, but the House Appropriations Committee reasoned that the center could return to private funding as it did prior to 1991. The center began restructuring in 2003, and the House cut $2 million that the center was expecting to receive.

In 1998, Sen. John McCain (R-Ariz.) ridiculed spending for both the East-West Center and the North-South Center: "I would not be at all surprised to see in next year's bill funding for a North-by-Northwest Center, perhaps to include a banquet room honoring the late Alfred Hitchcock."

$5.1 Million for the Mystic Seaport Maritime Museum in Mystic, Connecticut

Sen. Joseph Lieberman (D-Conn.) sponsored the first $1 million in fiscal year 1993 for the construction of the Mystic Seaport Maritime Education Center in Mystic.

Established in 1929, the center is the country's largest maritime museum and has received $5.1 million since fiscal year 1993 to construct and renovate projects at the Connecticut tourist attraction. In 1999, the museum received $1 million to build a year-round learning center that would provide education and research facilities to the public. Sen. Lieberman was excited to learn of the appropriation: "This funding will nurture the Seaport's growth, which is good news for the Mystic economy and for the Seaport's hundreds of thousands of annual visitors." At that time, it was estimated that for every $1 in public funding, the local economy could generate over $11 in economic growth annually.

The museum "annually serves over a million visitors" and charges an entrance fee of $12.00 per adult; $11.00 each for senior citizens, college students, and active military; and $6.00 per child (ages 6–12). The museum could have charged each visitor an extra dollar for five years and saved the taxpayers $5 million.

$1.25 Million for the Irish Institute at Boston College, Massachusetts

Established in 1997, the center works to promote "a more lasting peace on the island of Ireland" and "hosts officials and policymakers from Ireland and Northern Ireland for professional development programs in areas such as government, nonprofit, business, and education." According to its Web site, the institute "has an ongoing relationship with the American Ireland Fund and the International Fund for Ireland." Our money lies over the ocean.

$24.5 Million for the Asia Foundation in Washington, D.C., and San Francisco, California

The Asia Foundation is a nonprofit organization that promotes democracy and "a more open, peaceful, and prosperous Asia-Pacific region." While the House included $8.25 million in fiscal year 1999 for the Asia Foundation account, the Senate Appropriations Committee did not provide any money, stating "the Asia Foundation is a nongovernmental grant-making organization that Congress has repeatedly urged to aggressively pursue private funds to support its activities. The Committee believes that the time has come for the Asia Foundation to graduate from public support."

The organization receives generous contributions from many private foundations and corporations, including ChevronTexaco, the Levi Strauss Foundation, and the Pepsico Foundation, to name a few. Yet, from 1997 to 2000, Congress appropriated $24.5 million for the foundation. USAID, the World Bank, the National Endowment for Democracy, the East-West Center, and the U.S. Institute for Peace all work toward the same goal for the Asia-Pacific region.

$58 Million for Pacific Coastal Salmon Recovery

Added by the Senate in fiscal year 2000, the Pacific Coastal Salmon Recovery fund was established to assist state, tribal, and local salmon conservation and recovery efforts in Alaska, California, Oregon, and Washington. The House Appropriations Committee did not recommend funding for this program for several reasons: First, the authorization for the grant program under which this money was requested (Section VI of the Endangered Species Act) had expired; and second, funds were only allowed to be appropriated out of the Department of Interior, over which the Commerce subcommittee has no jurisdiction. Finally, there was no authorization for the payment of these funds as grants to these states. Thus, the House Committee concluded, "There are substantial questions about what the funds can be used for, who oversees the funds, the conditions under which the funds are provided, such that there is a need for authorizations to be pursued to at least set the ground rules for these funds." For a change, the Senate overrode these objections.

$1.1 Million for the Graveyard of the Atlantic Museum on Hatteras Island, North Carolina

In fiscal year 1999, Senate appropriator Lauch Faircloth (R-N.C.) added $750,000 for the Graveyard of the Atlantic Museum, a shipwreck museum planned for Hatteras Island on the Outer Banks. Since then, an additional $302,500 was added in fiscal years 2003 and 2004. The funds were channeled through the nonprofit Outer Banks Community Foundation and were contingent on a match from private sources. At the time of the 1999 appropriations, the $7.3 million project had been stalled for fifteen years while organizers struggled to keep up with the escalating size and cost projections. The museum was originally intended to be a place to display artifacts from the shipwreck of the famous U.S.S. *Monitor*, but the idea expanded to include artifacts from 1,000 ships that were wrecked off the coast of the Outer Banks.

Groundbreaking finally took place in December 1999. The museum's ship-like exterior and about half of the interior were constructed, and then the pool of funds dried up. An additional $2.2 million is still needed to complete construction of the 19,000 square foot museum, and NOAA refuses to relinquish the highly coveted *Monitor* artifacts until construction is finished. Nevertheless, the museum has opened for visitors. On an average day, a crowd of approximately 600 flows through the museum's doors, and on a rainy day, an estimated 1,000 visit.

According to the museum's Web site, "All donors of $10,000 and above will be commemorated with a plaque prominently displayed in the entrance of the new facility." Next to the commemorative plaque should be an inscription reminding taxpaying visitors that this project helped contribute to the $413 billion deficit.

$400,000 for the Institute of International Sport at the University of Rhode Island

Located in the state of House Commerce, Justice, State and the Judiciary Subcommittee Member Patrick J. Kennedy (D-R.I.), the institute was founded in 1986, in part "to promote ethical behavior and good sportsmanship on an international basis." Past pork was added for youth crime prevention and to support the Scholar-Athlete Games, which were first held at the university in 1993. Participating students are divided into ethnically and culturally diverse groups instead of divided into national teams. The 2004 Rhode Island Scholar-Athlete "Renaissance Experience" included competitions in sports, vocal performance, poetry, art, and "specialty contests like board games, spelling bee, scientific discovery and sports trivia, to name a few." It is unlikely that Ron Artest of the Indiana Pacers will be making any guest appearances.

$50,000 for Gang Prevention (i.e., Tattoo Removal Program) in San Luis Obispo, California

Gang prevention sounds like a noble cause, but digging deeper into the details of the project reveals it was added in 2002 by Rep. Lois Capps (D-Calif.) for a tattoo removal program in San Luis Obispo, California. The purpose was to assist local gang members who had changed their minds about tattoos they had once voluntarily added to their bodies. Somehow, their youthful indiscretion became the taxpayers' problem. The project had been receiving state funds during the time of the federal appropriation. Somebody should start an earmark removal program.

Defense: The Pigs Go Marching One by One

There is no arguing that defending the country is one of the few constitutional responsibilities of the federal government. As America's fighting men and women are sent to dangerous parts of the world, it would be nice to know that members of Congress are spending money on defense projects that help, not hinder, the ability to defend the nation.

In testimony before the Senate Armed Services Committee on June 28, 2001, Defense Secretary Donald Rumsfeld reaffirmed his commitment to the fiscal and physical defense of the country. He said, "We have an obligation to taxpayers to spend their money wisely. We need to ask ourselves: How should we be spending our taxpayer dollars? We are doing two things: First, we are not treating the taxpayers' dollars with respect—and by not doing so, we risk losing their support; and Second, we are depriving the men and women of our Armed Forces of the training, equipment, and facilities they need to accomplish their missions. They deserve better. We need to invest that money wisely."

CAGW couldn't agree more. Unfortunately, appropriators didn't listen to Secretary Rumsfeld.

$5 Million for the Design and Construction of a Parliament Building in the Solomon Islands

In 1991, Rep. Stephen Solarz (D-N.Y.) requested and received $5 million for the design and construction of a parliament building in the Solomon Islands. What this has to do with defense is anybody's guess. But many might remember Solarz as one of 17 members of Congress who had a little check-writing problem. The House of Representatives operated a bank that allowed members of Congress to knowingly run up an overdraft without any form of penalty. In 1992, the House Ethics Committee found that 300 Representatives—past and present—had bounced checks and that 17 members had run up an overdraft of more than $100,000, including Solarz, who had an overdraft (without financial penalties) of $594,646. Apparently, the congressman's financial excesses reached into the Department of Defense as well.

$25 Million for an Arctic Region Supercomputer

In 1993, Senate Defense Appropriations Subcommittee Ranking Member Ted Stevens (R-Alaska) grabbed $25 million for an Arctic region supercomputer, as part of a controversial and so far unsuccessful effort by the University of Alaska (UA) to trap energy from the aurora borealis. Now, the supercomputer is used for research on such Arctic topics as ocean and ice modeling, global climate modeling, weather forecasting, and enhanced topographic products from synthetatic aperture radar data.

The project, now known as the Arctic Region Supercomputing Center (ARSC), is still managed by the UA in Fairbanks. The center has abandoned its efforts to capture energy from the aurora borealis, and is currently updating the gargantuan computer system. The updated system will help the ARSC create a "supercomputing environment designed to help researchers learn more about salmon and whitefish populations in the Gulf of Alaska." It sounds like the ARSC is just fishing for justification to perpetuate its existence. But none of this will make the nation more secure.

$10 Million for a Grant to Marywood College in Scranton, Pennsylvania, to Study Military Stress on Families

In 1992, Rep. Joseph McDade (R-Pa.) snatched $10 million for an unauthorized grant to Marywood College in Scranton, Pennsylvania, to study military stress on families. This small Roman Catholic school, run by nuns of the Immaculate Heart of Mary, had an enrollment of nearly 3,000 in 1992. The $10 million grant was roughly one-third of the school's budget. The awarding of this study to Marywood baffled even the grant recipients.

To carry out the research, Marywood College established the

Military Family Institute, which published its 22-page report in November 1998, describing implementations that would help improve military family quality of life. That's $454,545.45 per page. Even worse, the Defense Department already has an Office of Quality of Life that provides overall services for military families.

$58 Million for the American Ship Building Company in Tampa, Florida

In 1993, Senate Defense Appropriations Subcommittee Chairman Daniel Inouye (D-Hawaii) and House Defense Appropriations Subcommittee Chairman John Murtha (D-Pa.) provided $58 million to bail out millionaire New York Yankee owner George Steinbrenner's American Ship Building Company in Tampa. The Navy and Maritime Administration opposed the payment, which was $20 million more than Steinbrenner was seeking in an ongoing lawsuit. Sen. Inouye and Rep. Murtha quietly added the money in conference. Steinbrenner's generous campaign contributions and the hiring of two lobbyists with close ties to both legislators helped. No wonder the Yankees can afford a $200 million payroll.

$40 Million for Bethlehem Steel's Sparrows Point, Maryland Shipyard

The Pennsylvania-based steel company was forced to file for bankruptcy in October 2001, due to increased overseas competition and less demand for steel products. The company proposed reducing labor and lowering wages and benefits in an attempt to cover the shortage. The United Steelworkers Union howled at the proposals, demanding immediate protection measures against steel imports, and $6 billion in federal funds to help cover retiree costs and federal loan guarantees. Senate appropriator Barbara Mikulski (D-Md.) lent the taxpayers' helping hand to her home state shipyard.

$15 Million for the World Cup USA 1994

The summer of 1994 marked the first time in the history of the World Cup that it was held outside Europe or South America. It was an attempt to help promote soccer, which is the most-loved sport worldwide. Revenues for the event were estimated in the $20 million range; organizers were pleased when the final tally brought in 150 percent more than estimated, or $50 million. Despite the multi-million dollar profit from the World Cup soccer games, the Senate in 1994 rejected by a vote of 21–77 an amendment requiring that the Department of Defense be reimbursed for expenses in support of profitable civilian sporting events.

Congress has been a big supporter of international sporting events. In 1995, the Senate dumped $17.4 million into the Defense Appropriations bill for other civilian sporting events, including $14.4 million for the Games of the XXVI Olympiad in Atlanta and $3 million for the Special Olympics in New Haven, Connecticut, for logistical support and personnel services.

Overall, the government spent $98 million on the 1996 summer games, $47 million of which came from the defense budget.

The Olympic games are a gold mine for advertisers. The 1996 Summer Olympics generated $1.7 billion in marketing revenues. The privileged few who attend the games are being subsidized by the rest of us taxpayers who have to watch endless hours of Bob Costas's commentary.

$10 Million for Brown Tree Snake Research

The Brown Tree Snake, which is found only in Guam, has not been discovered to be life-threatening to humans, nor does it have the ability to survive in North America. The snake was first introduced into Guam in the late 1940s. But the little Guam native continues to get under the skin of Sen. John McCain (R-Ariz.). Commenting on the numerous earmarks that found their way into the fiscal year 2005 Defense Appropriations Act, the senator zoned in on this earmark: "$1 million for the Brown Tree Snakes. Once again, the brown tree snake has slithered its way into our defense appropriation bill. I'm sure the snakes are a serious problem, but a defense appropriations act is not the appropriate vehicle to address this issue."

$15 Million for National Presto Industries in Eau Claire, Wisconsin

The Department of Defense (DOD) was resolutely against appropriating money until a lawsuit between DOD and National Presto Industries (NPI) was settled. The Eau Claire site was purchased in 1948 by NPI and was used to design and maintain manufacturing lines for artillery shells for the Army until 1980. The plant produced mass quantities of waste while producing such munitions. Although NPI claimed it followed waste disposal standards, the Environmental Protection Agency (EPA) found contamination in the waters and grounds near the plant.

Immediate contamination cleanup began, and because the plant was on "standby status" as a defense production site until 1992, DOD paid $5 million and EPA chipped in another $4 million. The company insisted that the government be held liable for cleanup costs, but DOD filed a lawsuit against NPI to reclaim the cleanup costs. Never assuming liability, the company agreed to repay the government $3.95 million in 1993 for cleanup costs.

Typical of Congress, appropriators doled out funds for the environmental remediation before a final legal resolution was reached. Even though the site is in Wisconsin, the Florida delegation pushed for the project because the company's headquarters is in Florida.

$4 Million for the Discovery Center of Science and Technology

Established in 1989, the Discovery Center of Science and Technology is a 501 (c) (3) nonprofit corporation dedicated to advancing science education in schools throughout northeastern Pennsylvania and northwestern New Jersey. According to the center's information Web site, "The Discovery Center began as a collaboration between Lehigh University, the Junior League of the Lehigh Valley, and the Bethlehem Junior Womans Club." Today it offers a variety of hands-on educational resources for inquiry-based learning while helping students meet new state science standards, but it does nothing to help our troops overseas.

$720 Million for an Additional DDG-51 Ship in Pascagoula, Mississippi

In 1998, Senate Majority Leader Trent Lott (R-Miss.) nabbed $720 million for an additional DDG-51 ship at the Ingalls Shipyard in his home state. Establishing a bad precedent, Sen. Lott secured funding for the assault ship without a Pentagon or House request. Sen. Lott's fondness for building ships may stem from the fact that the Ingall's shipyard, where it will be built, is literally within view of his backyard in Pascagoula. It also has sentimental value—Lott's father once worked at the shipyard. Although the Northrop Grumman-owned Ingalls facility is the largest private employer in the state of Mississippi, the amount of pork appropriated to the shipyard suggests it's a government-supported site. Commenting on the project, Sen. Lott quipped, "I'll do anything for that [Ingalls] shipyard."

$5 Million for the North Star Borough Landfill in Alaska

The borough is the second largest populated region in the state of Senate Appropriations Committee Chairman Ted Stevens (R-Alaska). According to the state's description of the location, "The Fairbanks North Star Borough's economy is healthy and growing. Since 1995, the personal income of workers in the economic base has increased 29 percent primarily due to increases in agriculture, mining, and federal government. . . . There is $118.6 million in federal and state capital improvement projects underway for schools, sewer and water projects, airports, utilities, and other structures." That equals $1,379.42 per capita for the borough's population of 85,978.

$3 Million for the Southern Observatory for Astronomical Research

According to an *Associated Press* report in January 1995, "The telescope will allow astronomers to peer back millions of years through time, something that's not possible in North Carolina or Brazil." As far as we know, it's not possible anywhere in the world. Yet, funds were procured to construct a state-of-the-art telescope high atop a mountain in northern Chile, South America. The astronomers at the University of North Carolina at Chapel Hill, the frontiersmen leading the exploration, hoped to travel through time by peering through the telescope lenses. The telescope would "return" from its galaxy quest with images of the universe as it was millions of years ago. Any chance there's some long-lost tax dollars out there?

$28.7 Million to the National Automotive Center (NAC) in Warren, Michigan

One of the research activities conducted by NAC involves a smart truck, about which Sen. John McCain (R-Ariz.) muses whether "the intellect of this truck will be such that it will not only be capable of heating up a burrito, but will also be able to perform advanced calculus while quoting Kirkegaard."

$17.9 Million for the Center for Excellence for Disaster Management & Humanitarian Assistance in Hawaii

According to its Web site, "The Center's mission is to promote effective civil-military management in international humanitarian

assistance, disaster response, and peacekeeping through education, training, research, and information programs." This sounds
a lot like other private and government organizations, including
USAID, the Red Cross, and Project HOPE, to name a few. But
Senate Defense Appropriations Subcommittee Ranking Member Daniel Inouye (D-Hawaii) has disastrously managed to add
tax dollars to this project in his home state.

$1 Million for the National Flag Foundation in Pittsburgh, Pennsylvania

The organization, located in the state of Senate Defense Appropriations Subcommittee Member Arlen Specter (R-Pa.), seeks
"to inspire people everywhere, but especially young people, to
have a greater respect for the flag," according to the foundation's director. Respect for the flag and country should start with
preserving our tax dollars for national security.

$500,000 for Minority Aviation Training at the William Lehman Aviation Center at Florida Memorial College in Florida

The center is located in the district of House appropriator Car-
rie Meek (D-Fla.), who explained in a 2000 press release that
the center will help develop minority aviators and skilled aviation
workers for the military and private sector. According to school

officials, the federal funds will provide scholarships for tuition, room, and board to 12 students. That's $41,000 per year per student, making Florida Memorial College more expensive than Harvard, Yale, or just about any other private, four-year undergraduate facility.

$121 Million for the Kaho'olawe Island Conveyance Fund in Hawaii

Since 1996, Senate Defense Appropriations Subcommittee Ranking Member Daniel Inouye (D-Hawaii) has grabbed $120.93 million for the Kaho'olawe Island Conveyance Fund. From 1941 to 1990, the Navy used the area for military exercises and disrupted the natural living situation for natives of the island. In 1980, the government worked out a deal to begin restoring the island; the 1991 defense appropriations bill established the Kaho'olawe Island Conveyance Commission to "negotiate" with Hawaii. No money was appropriated at the time for cleanup of the area, but Sen. Inouye has since made sure the taxpayers are burdened with the cost.

$3.7 Million for Math Teacher Leadership

How about this math problem? Congress has appropriated $3.65 million for a math teacher leadership project. Here is a simple math equation that doesn't need federal funds: In fiscal year 2001, there was $18.5 billion in pork-barrel spending, and Pentagon officials predicted an $18 billion shortfall in the defense budget to fight the war on terrorism.

$750,000 for the Center for Solar Geophysical Interactions at the Mt. Wilson Observatory in Pasadena, California

In 2002, the House threw $750,000 into a black hole for this project. An examination of the observatory's Web site did not describe any defense-related research. In January 2003, the Air Force Research Laboratory launched a similar project, the Solar Mass Ejection Imager. Typical of the government, the observatory project not only wastes defense appropriations funds on non-defense activities, but it also duplicates another government-funded project.

$3 Million for the Tanker Lease Pilot Program to Lease 100 Boeing 767 Re-fueling Tankers

A $3 million deal added in conference for the Tanker Lease Pilot Program to lease 100 Boeing 767 fuel tankers was tucked away in the fiscal year 2002 Defense Appropriations Act. The Government Accountability Office (GAO) estimated the cost of the six-year lease of the 100 tankers to be $26–$30 billion. As an alternative to the lease, GAO estimated the cost to upgrade, modernize, and repair corrosion to the current fleet of KC-135Es to be approximately $3.2 billion, a savings of more than $23 billion.

Sen. John McCain (R-Ariz.) was outraged by the proposal and pushed for an investigation of the bailout. He stated that "any program to acquire tankers must start from the beginning . . . on a traditional budget, procurement, and authorization track." Senate Armed Services Committee Chairman John W. Warner (R-Va.) sided with Sen. McCain, although many House members disagreed with the senator, including Rep. Norm Dicks (D-Wash.), whose district includes thousands of Boeing workers.

Federal investigations revealed that a Pentagon official, Air Force Procurement Officer Darleen A. Druyun, sweetened the Boeing deal as a "parting gift" before retiring from the Air Force and working for Boeing. The company fired her after e-mails were uncovered showing she negotiated her position while overseeing the company's work at the Air Force, including the tanker deal. The company's chief financial officer, Michael Sears, was also fired. Soon after Druyun's and Sears's dismissals, Boeing Chief Executive and Chairman Philip M. Condit resigned. On October 1, 2004, Druyun was sentenced to nine months in prison for inflating the tanker deal price before her retirement. On November 15, 2004, Sears pled guilty to a conflict-of-interest in the Boeing scheme and admitted that he arranged to hire Druyun while she was working at the Pentagon. Sears faces up to five years in prison.

Even though this deal was killed in the fiscal year 2005 Defense Appropriations Act, Boeing is keeping its fingers crossed that the arrangement will be revived, as the tanker leasing program is the only shot for the company to keep producing its 767 model.

$101 Million for the High Frequency Active Auroral Research Program (HAARP)

Initially designed to capture energy from the aurora borealis, HAARP is now being configured to heat up the ionosphere to improve military communications. Not surprisingly, HAARP is also heating up the ire of many taxpayers. When operations began on the DOD-owned property near the little town of Gakona, Alaska, local residents were alarmed by the project. According to a February 1997 *Science* article, "One person described seeing a mysterious 'green glow' above the site; another claimed that it was making caribou walk backward and having a 'mind-bending effect' on local residents." One enthusiast reported that DOD planned to construct a Star Wars-type missile shield and create a technological system to jam global communications.

Though HAARP is probably not building some menacing creation only seen in *Spider-Man* movies, many scientists call HAARP a "science fiction" project. In 1997, the University of Alaska's Geophysical Institute professor Syun-Ichi Akasofu stated that "to do what [has been talked] about, we would have to flatten the entire state of Alaska and put up millions of antennas, and even then, I am not sure it would work."

Despite all the criticism, Sen. Ted Stevens (R-Alaska) continued to funnel millions of dollars into the program. Web surfers can check out *www.haarp.alaska.edu* to see exactly how their tax dollars are being spent. Since 1995, CAGW has identified $100.9 million appropriated for HAARP.

$1 Million for the Young Patriots Program

According to the fiscal year 2004 Defense Appropriations Act Conference Report, this money will help to "expand the Young Patriots Program to include a video which promotes the significance of National Patriotic Holidays." Wouldn't it be more patriotic to just not spend this money?

$1 Million for Shakespeare in American Military Communities

According to the *Austin American-Statesman,* the program is "part of the National Endowment for the Arts Shakespeare in American Communities project to bring its work to unusual places. Ostensibly, this will get the troops' minds off war, fighting, and killing." Among the plays expected to be performed are *Macbeth* and *Othello,* two of the most violent and deadly plays written by Shakespeare.

District of Columbia: Inside the Beltway Pork

What is left to be said about the District of Columbia that hasn't already been said? The former mayor was caught smoking crack cocaine and won re-election as a member of the city council. And, the current mayor wants taxpayers to fund the construction of a new $584 million baseball stadium. It should come as no surprise that members of Congress found ample opportunity to fund some of their own pet projects. But, while Congress was worried about sufficient funding for the Frank Sinatra Museum, D.C. schools continued to deteriorate, and residents continued to flee the city likes rats from a sinking ship.

$300,000 for the Bicycle Improvement Project

In an effort to help the ever-increasing traffic jams around the Beltway, members of Congress began looking for ways to increase bicycle and public transportation commuters. In 1995, they appropriated $300,000 for the Bicycle Improvement Project. Advocates touted the health and cost benefits as well as the potential decrease in the amount of cars on the roadway. In 2003, *The Washington Post* reported that Maryland, Virginia, and D.C. spent another $1.64 million in federal funds to install bike racks on every Metro bus, offering another incentive for people to use bikes and public transportation to commute to work. That's a lot of money to increase the amount of bike commuters. In the Washington, D.C. region, less than 1 percent of the total of about 85,000 daily trips are done by bicycle, with three-fourths of those trips being for errands or recreation.

Why the city continues to fund a commuting option that doesn't appeal to the majority of the D.C. population is a mystery. Perhaps Congress should help fix the potholes as a way to help speed along the commute.

$300,000 for a National Museum of American Music Honoring Frank Sinatra

In a city with chronic deficits and crime, spending money on a Frank Sinatra Museum is an insult to every taxpayer in and out of D.C. In 2004 alone, Frank Sinatra's estate earned $5 million, and his total estate is determined to be worth between $200 to $600 million. Taxpayers are seeing red over Ol' Blue Eyes.

$3.45 Million for Brownfield Remediation at Poplar Point

President Clinton requested $10 million for this project, but the House denied funding because "the plan presented fails to provide any specific information as to the phases of the project, the start and completion dates and any detailed goals." Nevertheless, the Senate added $3.45 million for brownfield remediation at Poplar Point.

City planners have included restorations to Poplar Point in the Anacostia Waterfront Initiative. The point, which lies along the eastern shoreline of the Anacostia River, has been neglected for years but officials hope to renovate the spot to become "a showcase of ecological restoration, culture, history, and community," and "a catalyst for neighborhood economic development." To redevelop the ignored section of the river, numerous road construction projects must first be completed.

Because most of the land on the eastern side of the river is owned by the federal government, redeveloping Poplar Point will most likely be achieved using millions more taxpayer dollars in the future.

$500,000 for the Creation of the Kenilworth Regional Sports Complex

The Senate added this earmark in fiscal year 2002 for the Washington, D.C. Sports and Entertainment Commission, in coordination with the U.S. Soccer Foundation, for environmental and infrastructure costs at Kenilworth Park for creation of the Kenilworth Regional Sports Complex. Many private organizations already provide D.C. youth with venues for sports activities.

$1.75 Million for the City Museum

Funds were given to the Historical Society of Washington in fiscal year 2002 for capital improvements to the new City Museum, which was not scheduled to open until 2003. D.C. Council Chairwoman and museum supporter Linda Cropp said, "The new City Museum will showcase Washingtoniana—the history of the city, including its neighborhoods, citizens, schools, businesses, civic associations, and of course, politics and government."

In November 2004, the City Museum announced that it would close its doors due to $500,000 to $1 million in budget shortfalls, blaming the federal government for not providing enough funds. The historical society hopes to raise enough money to reopen the museum in 18 months. Part of the problem was that the museum lacked financial resources due to disinterest from the public. The museum was projected to have an estimated 100,000 visitors per year, but it never came close to that. In 2003, fewer than 40,000 visited the museum. Tickets were $5 for the general public and $4 for students. With 55 other museums in Washington, D.C., including the famous Smithsonian Museums and privately-owned International Spy Museum, it's no wonder the less-than-exciting City Museum had to shut down.

$1.1 Million for the Shakespeare Theatre

The Shakespeare Theatre received $1 million for the construction of a new downtown facility to provide affordable access to the arts and $125,000 for educational outreach programs. Tickets for Shakespeare productions cover about half of the costs of its $12 million operating budget. For the other half, the theatre relies on "more than 300 corporations, foundations, and public agencies along with more than 7500 individuals" to produce the necessary funds to keep the theatre operating. With so many corporate and private donors, Congress shouldn't be wasting funds on this project.

$1 Million for Barracks Row Main Street, Inc. for the Construction of Two Gateways

According to its official Web site, "The mission of Barracks Row Main Street is to revitalize 8th Street S.E. as a vibrant commercial corridor reconnecting Capitol Hill to the Anacostia waterfront. . . . Business is booming on 8th Street S.E., an award-winning model for community revitalization. It is a destination with a rich past, a bountiful present, and a bright future!" It would be nice if taxpayers had such a bright future.

$300,000 for Friends of Fort Dupont Ice Arena for Capital Improvements

This public skating rink rents ice time for individual skaters at a rate of $3 per hour; ice hockey teams, $220 per hour; and non-profits, $125 per hour. Birthday parties are also welcome. According to its Web site, the rink has "a long-standing proposal into the National Park Service to expand the facility to allow for another skating pad, new locker rooms and showers and other additional space needs." Just in case you want a souvenir to remember your trip, you can purchase one online: fleece blanket, $30.00; fleece vest, $10.00; a mug, $5.00; a stadium seat cushion, $5.00; a skate towel, $5.00; and a water bottle, $6.00. Cost to taxpayers? Priceless.

$8 Million for the Federal Payment for City Government Management Reform

With chronic deficits and mismanagement, it is the height of irony to think that the federal government should be giving money to the District of Columbia for management reform.

$7 Million for the Lorton Correctional Complex in Virginia

The House added this earmark for an environmental study at the then soon-to-be-closed complex, which was the federal government's facility for D.C. inmates. The jail was in or adjacent to the districts of House D.C. Appropriations Subcommittee Ranking Member Jim Moran (D-Va.), House Transportation Appropriations Subcommittee Chairman Frank Wolf (R-Va.), and House Government Reform D.C. Subcommittee Chairman Tom Davis (R-Va.), all of whom pushed for the project.

$19 Million for D.C. Public Charter School Facilities

Members of Congress added funds for D.C. public charter school facilities in fiscal year 2003. The earmark included $2 million for the SEED Foundation Charter School to construct an academic center and $12 million for CityBuild to create or expand charter schools in selected neighborhoods.

The District's publicly funded charter schools are generally free from the rules governing regular public schools. According to *The Washington Post,* "There is little evidence that they have done a better job on the whole than regular schools in raising student performance." The *Post* also notes that the city's charter schools have an enrollment of 14,007 students this school year. That means taxpayers paid $1,357 for students to choose a charter school when a public school was already available to them.

Instead of throwing money into new charter school facilities, D.C. should seek ways to eliminate the overspending occurring in the D.C. public school system. The District's local *ABC News Channel 7* reported in September 2004 that it had "uncovered a pattern of chronic over-spending and mismanagement that has cost taxpayers tens of millions of dollars" and "over the past five years, D.C. schools spent nearly $178 million more than they budgeted for school repairs and construction." Some examples of overspending over the last five years include:

- 🐷 Renovations to the northeast D.C. high school McKinley Tech, which went $29 million over budget;
- 🐷 Patterson Elementary School in southwest D.C., which went almost $16 million over budget;
- 🐷 A new facility, Barnard Elementary School in northwest D.C., which went $14 million over budget; and
- 🐷 Construction at the Kelly Miller School, which cost more than three times the original estimate; the original price tag was $10 million; final costs exceeded $34 million.

Energy and Water: The Power of Pork

On the surface, the Energy and Water Appropriations Act may seem as calm as a lake. In reality, this bill hides thousands of earmarks that members of Congress try to use in their reelection bids. In 1996, then-House Speaker Newt Gingrich (R-Ga.) urged appropriators to use the appropriations process to help Republicans get elected by insisting that "district items" be funded. One of the bills mentioned by name was the Energy and Water Appropriations Act.

One of the bill's favorite targets of pork is the Army Corps of Engineers, which has had a checkered past. The Secretary of the Army stamps a project "economically justified" whenever the predicted benefits are equal to or greater than the estimated costs. Such a low threshold is unwise and fails the common sense test. While many Army Corps projects and the process that implements them have been criticized for years, that scrutiny has increased since the Corps was the subject of a *Washington Post* article in February of 2000. The *Post* reported the agency had tried to squelch one of its most respected economists so that it could manipulate numbers and justify a billion-dollar navigation project on the Upper Mississippi River.

$115.5 Million to Continue the Red River Waterway to Shreveport, Louisiana

In 1991, Sen. J. Bennett Johnston (D-La.) grabbed $92.6 million just as he was facing a tough reelection. It was the largest single navigation project in the bill and represented 8 percent of all funds spent on water projects in fiscal year 1991. The administration had requested that the project end at Colfax (well short of Shreveport), but Sen. Johnston added two more locks.

Appropriations for the Red River didn't stop at the banks of Louisiana—it overflowed into just about every state in which the river runs. Dams and corridors have been built all along the winding river, along with chloride control projects and emergency bank protection.

The Red River Waterway connects the Mississippi to the Red River and extends upward in a northwestern direction from Old River to the Shreveport/Bossier City area. The project consists of a series of five locks and dams and a number of cutoffs to shorten the river. According to the U.S. Corps of Engineers, the "economic benefits from bank stabilization along this project are estimated at over $38 million annually. Navigational economic benefits are estimated at over $68 million annually at 1982 price levels."

However, the waterway has yet to justify the enormous amount of federal funding it has received. In 1997, only 4 percent of the projected commercial traffic that the U.S. Army

Corps of Engineers projected to justify the cost of the project meandered through the Red River Waterway. According to a January 9, 2000 *Washington Post* article, "The Red still carries less than 0.1 percent of the commercial traffic on America's government-run river transport system—even though it receives a remarkable 3.4 percent of the system's federal funds." In 2003, the U.S. Army Corps of Engineers said the $2 billion worth of construction costs won't be justified until 2046.

According to Dr. Robert Sterns, an economist at the University of Maryland and formerly a top official with the Army Corps, "The story of the Red River is important . . . because it is the most recent expensive new waterway and suggests the limited benefits of expensive barging projects on similar smaller rivers today." A 2000 Environmental Defense Fund report found that "taxpayers pay the vast majority of the costs of constructing and maintaining barge waterways. . . . Because these projects cause significant harm to fish and wildlife, they certainly should not be built when they do not even make sense economically."

Since much of Red River Waterway pork has barged through the appropriations bills thanks to Sen. Johnston, the project was renamed the "J. Bennett Johnston Waterway" in 2001.

$220.7 Million for the Appalachian Regional Commission (ARC) to Continue Work on Two Corridor Construction Projects

The ARC was created in 1965 as a temporary response to poverty in Appalachia, but today it serves primarily as an expressway for pork. This federal-state "partnership" annually drains money from the federal coffers to finance various programs, which, according to the ARC Web site, "create thousands of new jobs" and "bring more of Appalachia's people into America's economic mainstream."

The ARC was blessed with two generous earmarks in the 1994 Energy and Water Appropriations Act. One earmark was slipped in by the Senate for a $50 million Corridor L road construction project in West Virginia, home to Appropriations Committee Chairman Robert Byrd (D-W.Va.). The other 1994 ARC road construction project was added in conference for $38.7 million worth of work in the state of House appropriator Tom Bevill (D-Ala.). The pork highway didn't stop there—an additional $54 million for Appalachian Corridor construction projects was added in the 1994 Transportation Appropriations bill.

CAGW has tracked $220.7 million for pork-barrel construction projects inserted into Energy Appropriations bills from 1994 to 2004. From Alabama to Kentucky to New York, Congress paved the way through the Appalachian Mountains by appropriating billions of taxpayer dollars to construct the 26 highway corridors. The 13 states that make up the Appalachian Corridor have all received funding through the ARC, though West Virginia has been the major beneficiary of corridor construction, thanks to Sen. Byrd. In 1997, Corridor L received money to upgrade to four lanes at the cost of $287 million in state and federal funds. The taxpayer cost of creating Corridor L alone is $461 million.

In 1996, *Appalachia Magazine,* ARC's journal, reported that "Senator Byrd added funds to a federal appropriations bill to help communities along the highway capitalize on existing tourism opportunities and attract new tourism-related busi- nesses and jobs." West Virginia Governor Gaston Caperton added, "Completing these arteries, such as Appalachian Corri- dor L, opens regions to enormous economic development and tourism opportunities, and that means more jobs and progress for West Virginians. We can thank Senator Byrd for his relent- less effort to help communities along Corridor L and to maintain the Appalachian Development Highway System."

$20.4 Million for the Department of Energy's Advanced Liquid Metal Reactor

The Senate added this $20.4 million earmark in the 1994 Energy and Water Appropriations Act, despite a 1993 House vote to kill the project. Termination of the Advanced Liquid Metal Reactor (ALMR) would have saved $318 million over five years. The ALMR is the reincarnation of the Clinch River Breeder Reactor Program, which explored the concept of a nuclear reactor capa- ble of breeding plutonium. Eliminating that program in 1983 didn't halt Congress's fascination with the idea of breeding plu- tonium.

When Congress began to explore the possibility of breeding plutonium at the expense of taxpayers, numerous independent scientists warned against the idea. According to the Electric Power Research Institute in 1991, "The policy would likely incur a large cost penalty, encounter major institutional difficulties, multiply licensing difficulties, and amplify political and public op-

position to the nuclear power program as a whole." Frans
Berhout, an energy materials and nuclear weapons expert, argued in 1992 that "proponents of nuclear power sometimes argue that military plutonium should be stored to provide start-up
fuel for fast-neutron plutonium breeder reactors when they
eventually become commercially feasible; however, that argument makes little sense. . . . They are not even close to being
cost-effective."

Attempting to trim the federal budget deficit, the House voted
to cut this project. Supporting outside recommendations to terminate ALMR, the House stated that "independent scientific experts believe that liquid metal reactors would greatly increase
the cost of radioactive waste disposal and would not provide
significant environmental benefits" and "arms control experts
believe that liquid metal reactors raise grave nuclear prolifera-
tion concerns because of the potential for production of plutonium through breeding and reprocessing." Despite all the
warnings against funding ALMR, the Senate just couldn't resist
advancing millions toward this uncertain program.

ALMR has cost taxpayers $1.3 billion since 1986. Though
the program only received the one-time earmark, the Department of Energy continues to support risky and unsafe plutonium
breeding projects.

$1.85 Million to Three Independent Commissions: the Delaware River Basin Commission, the Susquehanna River Basin Commission, and the Interstate Commission on the Potomac River

In the 1931 Delaware River Diversion case, U.S. Supreme Court Justice Oliver Wendell Holmes asserted that "a river is more than an amenity; it is a treasure." Digging into its own treasure coffers—the taxpayers' wallets—the Senate appropriated $1.85 million to three independent commissions in 1996: $771,000 for the Delaware River Basin Commission; $568,000 for the Susquehanna River Basin Commission; and $511,000 for the Interstate Commission on the Potomac River Basin. These three commissions already receive state and federal contributions through the Clean Water State Revolving Fund (CWSRF) program, which provides low interest rates and flexible loans for funding estuary protection and other measures to protect the environment.

Including the one-time earmarks in 1996 for the three commissions, projects along the Delaware River, the Potomac River, and the Susquehanna River have received $15,291,000 in appropriations since 1991.

The Delaware River Basin Commission (DRBC) was established in 1961 when President Kennedy and the governors of Delaware, New Jersey, New York, and Pennsylvania signed into law legislation that created a regional body with the force of law to oversee a unified approach to managing a river system. Today, the commission's programs include "water quality protection, water supply allocation, regulatory review (permitting), water conservation initiatives, watershed planning, drought management, flood control, and recreation."

Since 1996, Congress has channeled $9,048,000, including the $771,000 for the DRBC, into projects along the Delaware River. It's no wonder why the four states that share the river are interested in keeping the funds flowing. According to *The Philadelphia Inquirer*, "The U.S. Maritime Administration reported that goods valued at $26.7 billion flow along the river. Shad fishing alone is a multimillion-dollar enterprise on the Delaware, and there are many notable trout streams in the watershed, along with numerous locations for boating and other water-sport recreation."

The Susquehanna River Basin Commission (SRBC) operates much in the same way as does the DRBC. The SRBC grew from the 1970 Susquehanna River Basin Compact, which involved the state legislatures of Maryland, New York, and Pennsylvania and provided guidelines for conservation and administration of the water resources of the river basin. Including the $568,000 allotted in 1996 for the SRBC, the Susquehanna River has received $4,187,000 for projects, plus an additional $175,000 split between the Susquehanna and Delaware Rivers for U.S. Army Corps of Engineers' developments.

Sen. Arlen Specter (R-Pa.) has long championed funding for the Susquehanna River. The river runs through Rep. Paul E. Kanjorski's (D-Pa.) district, and the congressman has pushed hard to receive federal funding for the Susquehanna Riverfront Project, which is designed to revitalize the Wilkes-Barre section of the river to a "recreation destination." According to a 2004 press release from Rep. Kanjorksi's office, plans for the project include "public access to the River for fishing and boating, a 1.2

acre plaza, walking trails, and an amphitheater for outdoor festivals and performances." Also, "while total costs are still being calculated, it is expected that the majority of the project costs will be borne by the federal government." Preserving our waterways may be of national significance, but pouring millions of appropriations dollars into a tourist attraction project should be left to the state that benefits, not taxpayers.

The Interstate Commission on the Potomac River Basin (ICPRB) is an interstate compact organization composed of the District of Columbia, Maryland, Pennsylvania, Virginia, and West Virginia. The ICPRB was established in 1940 to regulate and prevent pollution of the Potomac River by sewage and industrial wastes. The river experiences a high volume of annual recreational use. For instance, in 1998, recreation and tourism in the Potomac headwaters generated an annual $205 million for West Virginia's economy. CAGW has tracked $1,881,000 in federal funding toward restoration activities of the Potomac River since 1993.

$9.5 Million for the Energy, Minerals, and Materials Research Center at the University of Alabama

House Energy and Water Appropriations Subcommittee Ranking Member Tom Bevill (D-Ala.) certainly had reason to push for the $9.5 million for the Energy, Minerals, and Materials Research Center at the University of Alabama. The university is not only his alma mater, but the new $20 million Tom Bevill Energy,

Mineral, and Material Science Research Building was named in honor of Rep. Bevill's generous "donation."

$7 Million for Construction and River Levee Work at the Louisiana State Penitentiary

It's criminal the way appropriators throw taxpayer money into unnecessary construction projects. The project, in the state of then–House Appropriations Committee Chairman Robert Livingston (R-La.), has helped create a unique and crafty atmosphere at the prison. In 1998, the same year that Congress appropriated money for "general construction" at the working prison, the Louisiana State Penitentiary Museum was established to "preserve its prolific past and to educate the general public about the role this sprawling prison has played in [Louisiana] state's history." At the museum, visitors can see guards' weapons and view an authentic electric chair. Tourists who wish to remember their unique trip to the Louisiana State Penitentiary can purchase crafts and other gifts made by the inmates—at the tourists' (taxpayers') expense.

$7.75 Million for the Gridley Rice Straw Project

In the 1990s, California farmers were forced to stop routine burning of their rice fields to help reduce smog in urban areas.

As an alternative way of disposing of the rice straw, farmers had the idea of building an ethanol brewery in Gridley, California, which would turn the rice into ethanol. However, rice farmers realized that turning rice into ethanol wasn't nearly as easy as using corn kernels. The Gridley plant was expected to turn an estimated 140,000 tons of rice straw into ethanol per year, in order to replace the dependence on corn-based fuel from the Midwest. Yet, the first batch of ethanol production didn't produce enough to compensate farmers for the time-consuming process. Still, a $20 million facility is being built to house this flop of a project, and is expected to open in 2006.

$6 Million for the Million Solar Roofs Initiative

The Million Solar Roofs Initiative (MSRI) was not originally a Department of Energy (DOE) project; rather, it started out as an announcement in 1997 by President Clinton during an address to the United Nations. The House Committee scoffed at the idea, as members believed the cost of the program would not be worth it. They were right. A DOE press release in 1998 announced an award of $5 million to select business ventures to install a thousand solar systems. Assuming DOE estimates were correct, each roof system would cost $32,000 on average, $5,000 of which would be paid by taxpayers. The committee was sufficiently concerned about the taking of taxpayer funds for this venture that it warned the administration not to show off the program, urging DOE to "use lowercase letters when touting the goal of outfitting one million solar roofs." Despite the recommendation by the House, the program was awarded $1.5 million in conference in 1999, according to a Capitol Hill source, simply to see how the money would be spent.

To achieve one million solar energy roofs on U.S. buildings by 2010, MSRI includes two types of solar technology: photovoltaics, which produce electricity from sunlight, and solar thermal systems, which produce heat for hot water, space heating, or heating swimming pools. The MSRI Web site promises, "The Initiative will not direct and control the activities at the state and local level, nor will it typically pay for the installation of solar energy systems." Yet, the program has been awarded $6 million since 1999.

The MSRI Web site also claims the initiative is helping to keep the U.S. solar energy industry competitive in the global marketplace. Why Congress assumes it needs to assist the solar energy industry is a mystery; by 2005, the photovoltaic market alone is expected to exceed $1.5 billion worldwide.

$1.3 Million for the National Wind Technology Center in Boulder, Colorado

Located in the district of former House appropriator David Skaggs (D-Colo.) in Boulder, Colorado, the center "is a place where government scientists work side-by-side with U.S. industry to create advanced wind systems of the future." NWTC has worked for two decades to reduce the costs associated with

the wind energy industry, and according to the center's calculations, wind power *could* supply 20 percent of the electricity in
the U.S.

Private energy companies like General Electric are already
investing in wind energy technology. In 2003, the company
raked in nearly $18.5 billion in total revenues and is one of the
leading manufacturers of wind power worldwide.

$130 Million for the Denali Commission

Congressional members can't resist establishing commissions in
order to funnel millions of taxpayer dollars to their home states.
From 2000 to 2003, $130 million was appropriated to Senate
Appropriations Committee Chairman Ted Stevens' (R-Alaska)
pet project, the Denali Commission. Initially established to funnel
federal economic development aid to Alaska, the organization
has expanded to cover federal assistance for building hospitals,
healthcare centers, and other medical facilities. Sen. Stevens
created the commission in 1998 and has been its only champion
in the annual budget free-for-all.

In 2000 and 2001, the House Appropriations Committee didn't
give the commission any money, seeking to terminate its work
and to retrieve $18 million in unspent 1999 funds. Yet Sen.
Stevens stared down his House counterparts and sought $25
million for the commission. He was disappointed when it only
received $20 million. "We'll have to live with it," the senator told
the press. "Some of the reductions come about because I am

chairman [of the Appropriations Committee]. Some think the money wouldn't be there if I weren't chairman." Only *some*?

Although Sen. Stevens sneaked $130 million into past appropriations bills, federal funding for the Denali Commission doesn't stop there. The commission receives a smorgasbord of funds from numerous federal departments. For instance, in 2003, the commission was expected to receive $18 million under the U.S. Department of Agriculture's Rural Electrification Act, which was amended to include the commission; the Department of Health and Human Services chipped in another $27.5 million; and the Environmental Protection Agency "owed" the commission an estimated $3 million for sewer, power, and bulk fuel storage projects.

Despite this enormous amount of funding, the commission hopes to soon see funding for transportation projects throughout Alaska. Facing a tough reelection in 2004, Sen. Lisa Murkowski (R-Alaska), with the help of Sen. Stevens, pushed transportation legislation through the Senate, which includes funding a "new" commission, the Denali Transportation Commission, at a level of $180 million over the next six years to improve Alaska's rural roads.

$12 Million for the Vermont Gasification Project

This project, located in Burlington in the state of Senate appropriator Patrick Leahy (D-Vt.), received appropriations even though the House Appropriations Committee explicitly prohibited further funding. The gasification project, also known as the McNeil Biomass Project, began a decade ago to develop a heating system which uses "renewable resources"—a mixture of steam, recycled hot sand, and wood chips. Initially, capital costs to develop the system were expected to be low, yet the project experienced many problems while attempting to modernize the heating system.

The Department of Energy (DOE) has been funding the system since 1994. Despite some success of the project in 1998, the DOE inspector general (IG) stated that the McNeil project was "inadequate," despite receiving more than $36 million from DOE in fiscal years 2001 and 2002. A December 2003 IG report on the "defunct" project found that "no additional milestones were achieved," and the project was forced to shut down in October 2001. However, the IG report noted that "the department continued to provide reimbursements up until one day before the financial assistance recipient filed for protection under Chapter 11 of the bankruptcy code."

$4 Million for the Sealaska Corporation Ethanol Project Near Ketchikan, Alaska

In both 2001 and 2002, Senate Appropriations Committee Chairman Ted Stevens (R-Alaska) nabbed $2 million for the native-owned Sealaska Corporation to continue the Southeast Alaska Bioenergy Project (SABP). The $4 million of pork will help build a wood-to-ethanol plant to turn Alaska's southeast old-growth (Tongass) timber and timber scraps into ethanol for use as a gasoline additive. The creation of this $43 million ethanol production facility near Ketchikan "would produce six million gallons of ethanol annually and create a significant number of direct jobs and indirect jobs in Alaska."

Corn grain is the common feedstock for ethanol because it's easy to ferment and distill. The Midwest supplies Alaska's ethanol demands of roughly 4 million gallons per year. Sealaska-sponsored studies estimate that the Ketchikan plant would produce approximately 6 million gallons of ethanol annually, removing Alaska's dependency on the Midwest's ethanol.

Though Sealaska just recently found itself a recipient of Sen. Stevens's generous gift of taxpayer dollars, the wood-to-ethanol project began several years ago, and since its inception has experienced many problems. As the *Alaska Journal of Commerce* reported in May 2004, "The wood residue available in Southeast Alaska contains much more bark than previously anticipated." This is a major roadblock, since a December 2001 report on the project stated that ethanol yield decreases as the bark content of the wood increases. The scraps used in the Alaska demonstration include chunks of bark, making the project less efficient than expected. Because SABP is moving at a much slower and less successful rate than anticipated, the new cost estimates for the project, which were supposed to be released in late 2004, will most likely be much higher than the original estimates.

Conservation activists rail against this corporate welfare giveaway. In a 2003 Southeast Alaska Conservation Council report, Scott Trainum, an ethanol plant expert, stated that "since 1982, American taxpayers have lost almost one billion dollars on the Tongass timber program," which includes the wood-to-ethanol plant proposed by Sealaska. He concluded, "According to my calculations, using a current interest rate, this plant will fail to make a profit."

Despite Trainum's warnings, the plans for the ethanol plant are still underway. It appears that no matter what experts in energy conservation say, Sen. Stevens is determined to continue spending millions in taxpayer dollars to build his ethanol plant in Alaska.

$5 Million for the Life Sciences Building at Brown University

Congressional members love to toss taxpayer money toward building facilities at renowned universities. For instance, in 2001, House appropriator Patrick J. Kennedy (D-R.I.) and Senate appropriator Jack Reed (D-R.I.) secured this $4 million for Brown University, which happened to be in Rep. Kennedy's district. In 2003, the project received an additional $1 million for continued development of the Life Sciences Building. At that time, Brown's endowment was $1.44 billion, which means the university would have only had to use 0.07 percent of those funds to support this project.

The total cost of the 168,800-square-foot building is $95 million. The College Hill Neighborhood Association stated that "Brown is receiving several million dollars from the Federal government towards construction costs." Perhaps in the future, taxpayers can help support other universities in need, such as Harvard, Yale, or Stanford.

$12.2 Million to Combat Erosion of Indiana's Shoreline

Since 1996, Congress has shoveled more than $12.2 million into this project, located in the district of House Energy and Water Appropriations Subcommittee Ranking Member Peter Visclosky (D-Ind.). Michigan City harbor structures have caused sand erosion along the Indiana Dunes National Lakeshore, specifically near Mt. Baldy. To replenish the shoreline, the U.S. Army Corps of Engineers will truck sand in from an "approved inland source" at five-year intervals for the next 50 years. The project is expected to cost $184 million "at 100 percent federal expense." The usual division is 75 percent federal and 25 percent state funding.

Rep. Visclosky touted his success at securing funding for Indiana's shoreline in a 2003 press release: "We would provide greater opportunities for individuals and families to experience a day at the beach in the Indiana Dunes, the crown jewel of northwest Indiana. By making this natural wonder even more attractive, we can improve the quality of life for everyone in our region. . . . Nearly two million tourists come to our region each year to enjoy the dunes . . . and they provide support to local businesses and the region's economy. It is vital that we preserve and enhance this natural treasure, and I will keep working hard to secure as much funding as possible for the Indiana Dunes." Clearly, Rep. Visclosky does not care about the erosion of taxpayers' money for his pet project.

$8.8 Million for the North Padre Island Packery Channel

In 2004, Senate appropriator Kay Bailey Hutchison (R-Texas) sailed away with $3 million for the North Padre Island Packery Channel. The plans for this Texas project call for dredging a channel through a popular beach on the island that would link the Laguna Madre to the Gulf of Mexico via the Packery Channel. It will take an estimated $30 million to complete the project, which will help developers transform part of the barrier island into a resort. Plans for the renovated island include beachside hotels, shops, restaurants, and other amenities including a golf course and an amusement park. According to the *Amarillo Globe News*, "Scientists and residents said the new project would benefit only a handful of wealthy [North Padre Island, Texas] residents." Taxpayers have contributed $8,836,000 since 2001 to this Texas resort destination.

$50 Million for an Indoor Rainforest in Coralville, Iowa

In 2004, Senate Finance Committee Chairman Charles Grassley (R-Iowa) added in conference perhaps the most ridiculed project since Boston's Big Dig—$50 million for an indoor rainforest project in Coralville, Iowa. The project was originally included in the Energy Policy Act of 2003 bill that failed to pass in December 2003. The Iowans for Responsible Development, critics of the project, celebrated when the rainforest was dropped from the energy bill: "It is good news for us, good news for Iowa City and Coralville . . . it was a very mistaken project."

But the celebration was short-lived. Taxpayers were still burdened with the indoor Amazon. The rainforest was apparently so indispensable that Sen. Grassley added it to the fiscal year 2004 Consolidated Appropriations Act in late January 2004.

When it is completed, Iowa will have the world's largest enclosed rainforest, spanning five acres. The enormous 20-story enclosure will look like a giant foil-covered caterpillar bordering Interstate 80. Scenery for the indoor natural wonder include suspended wooden bridges 100 feet in the air, hundreds of towering Brazilian beautyleaf, and American mahogany trees. Tourists will be able to wander among a myriad of activity centers, such as an aquarium, the rainforest, learning stations, and possibly an IMAX-style theater in what the *Des Moines Register* describes as "a kind of prairie-meets-the-Amazon setting."

A local businessman, Ted Townsend (heir to the Townsend meat-packing fortune), came up with this idea while contemplating his legacy on a treadmill. Since then, Townsend has worked to see that taxpayers will pay dearly for his dream to be realized. Original projections put the cost of the rainforest at $300 million; the project was scaled back to a more "reasonable" $225 million when it was included in the 2004 omnibus bill. The project is currently estimated to cost $180 million; Townsend has pledged a generous $10 million. However, the project is still $90 million short, and it must attract 1.1 million visitors annually to pay for itself. Although U.S. taxpayers are being drained $50 million for the "federal energy grant" and Coralville is adding

$15 million for land for the complex, no local governments are financing the project.

Water recycling and energy conservation have been promised once the project is completed. Other than claiming the project will be an "ecological inspiration" and will utilize "environmentally focused systems," no environmental benefits of building an indoor rainforest have been outlined.

This tropical boondoggle has some big-name supporters, such as former Iowa Governor Bob Ray (R), who is the chairman of the institute Townsend founded to oversee the production of the rainforest. Ray imagines that it will solve the state's "demographic problems" by drawing more people to move to Iowa. Ray also believes that mass quantities of retiring baby boomers will "crisscross the country" to visit the indoor rainforest. Sen. Grassley claims that it will somehow help the University of Iowa.

Optimists expect Iowa's project to pump $187 million a year into Coralville's economy, and to turn into a "defining tourism destination," which the state currently lacks. David Oman, project director for the Iowa Environmental Project (the official name of the rainforest), hopes to attract travelers on "I-80 or I-380 en route to other destinations." Oman's plan is very ambitious, since according to consultants, most travelers (57 percent) come to Iowa to visit relatives and friends; only a few (10 percent) come for entertainment.

Outside experts are dubious that Iowa's rainforest will draw 1.1 million tourists per year to Coralville. According to the *Des Moines Register*, "Critic Eileen Robb wrote . . . 'Perhaps the best that Iowans can hope for is that [the Iowa Environmental Project] will be purchased for pennies on the dollar in the future and put to a rational economic use, as happened in March 2003 to Colorado's Ocean Journey. The bankrupt $93 million Denver aquarium was recently purchased for just $13.6 million by Landry's seafood restaurant chain. Folks in Denver will now be able to watch their fish and eat them, too.' "

Raising the final $90 million to begin work on the rainforest may be the least of Oman's worries. According to industry officials, attractions need to continually expand or add new features or else attendance will drop dramatically. Supporters say they haven't focused on the next stages, but plans call for an expansion five years after the projected 2008 opening.

Andrew Grossman, editor of The Heritage Foundation's *Insider Magazine*, heavily criticized Grassley's rainforest project and warned taxpayers not to be surprised "if Texas wins funding for an indoor glacier park in the 2005 budget." Ultimately, this project will do nothing for Iowa's population, energy industry, or the environment, but it will soak the taxpayers.

Foreign Operations: When Pigs Fly . . . Overseas

As the world copes with the devastation caused by the tsunami disaster in the Indian Ocean, Americans and their government are generously providing hundreds of millions of dollars in relief. That is the positive side of foreign aid. On the dark side is the tidal wave of pork projects that have been added to the foreign aid appropriations bills, money that could have been used to save lives instead of protecting the incumbency of members of Congress.

$290.4 Million for the International Fund for Ireland

Talk about the luck of the Irish. The International Fund for Ireland (IFI) has been a pet project for Congress since its inception in 1986. In support of the Anglo-Irish Agreement, the fund was established by the Irish and British governments for two main purposes: "To promote social and economic advance and to encourage contact, dialogue and reconciliation between nationalists and unionists on the island of Ireland." Monies that support IFI come from five sources: the United States, the European Union, Canada, Australia, and New Zealand.

The "Four Horsemen"—House Speaker Tip O'Neill (D-Mass.), Sen. Edward Kennedy (D-Mass.), Sen. Daniel Patrick Moynihan (D-N.Y.), and New York Governor Hugh Carey (D)—championed support for Northern Ireland, including U.S. monetary contributions to IFI. The U.S. contribution to IFI is to be spent on "those projects that hold the greatest potential for job creation and equal opportunity for the Irish people." In 1991, as a parting gift for Speaker O'Neill, Congress gave $20 million to the fund. The funding fueled significant projects such as an "all Ireland genealogy project" and two pony-trekking centers; it also helped Boston stores sell crafts from Northern Ireland.

Former House Speaker Thomas Foley (D-Wash.) supported further funding of IFI, and the fiscal year 1993 Foreign Aid Appropriations Act stated that "the United States government has identified two priorities in its contribution to the fund: job creation and the leveraging of additional investment into the economy. . . . It is apparent that the number of worthy projects will exceed the amount appropriated by Congress for fiscal year 1992 and that a further U.S. contribution could be productively used."

Millions of taxpayer dollars continue to flow from Congress into IFI coffers. In 2001, two examples of IFI spending included the reopening of Walsh's Hotel in Maghera and opening the Sligo Fold Park in Riverstown, which features a restored farmhouse and an agricultural museum. Projects funded in the past have included building a replica of the *Jeanie Johnston* (a Canadian ship that once ferried famine victims across the Atlantic), a national water sports center used for coaching top-level athletes, golf videos, and exporting sweaters.

Since 1986, IFI has spent nearly $483.5 million to achieve its goals; the U.S. contribution of $290.4 million is 60 percent of that amount.

$3.65 Million for the United States Telecommunications Training Institute (USTTI)

The real purpose of USTTI is to increase the foreign markets of the multi-billion dollar telecommunications industry, which can certainly do without the generous yearly congressional support. According to *Research and Markets 2004 Telecommunications Review and Forecast*, "While segments of the U.S. telecom industry have faced intense economic challenges, overall spending in the U.S. rose by 4.9 percent in 2003. . . . Over the 2004–2007 period, the U.S. telecommunications industry will increase at a projected 9.2 percent compound annual rate, rising to $1 trillion."

After the initial $650,000, Congress has appropriated $500,000 annually thereafter, totaling $3.65 million from 1996 to 2003 in support of USTTI's global mission. The $3.65 million Congress allotted to USTTI is .0036 percent of the telecommunications industry's projected profits—proving the industry could have found a way other than taxpayer money to support its global expansion.

$15.7 Million for the International Fertilizer Development Center (IFDC)

Since 1997, Congress has shoveled $15.7 million to the IFDC. Headquartered in Muscle Shoals in the state of Senate Foreign Operations Appropriations Subcommittee Member Richard Shelby (R-Ala.). IFDC was founded in 1974 with the vision of helping in "the quest for global food security." Although the fight against world hunger is an important cause, this program duplicates the output of many government agencies, which already funnel resources into similar research projects and programs.

IFDC began receiving international attention after the 1995 terrorist bombings in Oklahoma City, Oklahoma, which were implemented by the use of explosives made from ammonium nitrate fertilizer. The Muscle Shoals facility was asked to research how the world's food supply would be impacted if production of ammonium nitrate was banned, and research the types of fertilizer used for explosives.

Sen. Jeff Sessions (R-Ala.) praised the project, most likely because the center employs many Alabama residents: "I believe it is one of the most effective programs our government has to improve the world. Dollar for dollar, there is nothing we do that will ease world hunger more than teaching underdeveloped nations modern farming techniques and how to wisely use fertilizer."

In 1997, earmarks for IFDC began to appear, and the facility's president and CEO Amit H. Roy accredited former Sen. Howell Heflin (D-Ala.) and Senators Shelby and Sessions with securing the new funding.

Sen. Shelby has made sure this pungent project receives

funds again in fiscal year 2005: "I'm very pleased that the Senate once again recognized the merits of [IFDC]. . . . In addition to the important research conducted at this facility, the facility employs numerous Muscle Shoals-area residents." And it takes tax dollars from numerous non-Muscle Shoals-area residents.

And we thought all the fertilizer research was being conducted on Capitol Hill.

$1.2 Million for the Mitch McConnell Conservation Fund

The fund, named after Kentucky's senior Sen. Mitch McConnell (R), promotes conservation of biodiversity and sustainable development of the province of the Galapagos Islands, because "Ecuador does not have the resources to assure the laws are implemented." In fiscal year 1999, $1.2 million was earmarked for the fund: $500,000 was allocated for the Charles Darwin Research Station; $200,000 was earmarked for activities conducted by the Galapagos National Park Service; and $500,000 was to be contributed to an endowment for the Charles Darwin Research Station and Foundation.

Ironically, 14 years ago, Sen. McConnell was one of the main crusaders against U.S. foreign aid. He believed USAID should be completely eliminated or transferred to the State Department. But when he became chairman of the Senate Foreign Operations Appropriations Subcommittee, his tune changed. According to *The Washington Post,* "McConnell has used that position to channel aid money to Kentucky contractors, such as the University of Louisville and Western Kentucky University, and to favored environmental causes, such as the Mitch Mc-Connell Conservation Fund." After the 1999 endowment from the Mitch McConnell Conservation Fund, the Charles Darwin Foundation named the fund a "permanent and long-term source" of revenue for the foundation. Looks like the U.S. tax-payers have bought into Darwin's theories for life.

$43 Million for the Russian Far East Program

This corporate welfare giveaway will help American firms with expertise in primary industries, including natural resource development, telecommunications, basic infrastructure, finance, and consumer goods, expand their markets to the Russian Far East. There are currently other government programs trying to achieve the same goals. For example, the Overseas Private Investment Corporation supports and promotes U.S. private investment in developing countries, including Russia; the Export-Import Bank "has been actively pursuing financing opportunities" in Russia for the past decade and leverages approximately $150 million annually into the Russian economy.

$30 Million for the Russian Leadership Program

Also known as the Open World Leadership Program, it was proposed in early 1999 by the U.S. Library of Congress, and backed by Rotary International and the United Methodist Church's Board of Global Ministries. The purpose of this program is to expose emerging leaders in the Russian Federation to the U.S. economic system, democratic institutions, people, and culture.

Three thousand Russian political, business, and community leaders flew to the U.S. as part of this program in September 1999 to participate in activities such as a visit to the Festival Flea Market in Florida, a trip to the Coors brewery in Colorado, and a swing dance. During the 2004 trips, Russians were able to take in the scenic sites of the Southwest, the fields of the Heartland, and the southern charms of Alabama, among other U.S. attractions. In Rover Park, New Mexico, delegates were able to attend a Republican Party BBQ dinner; in Beatrice, Nebraska, Russians worked with local 4-H clubs; and Russian jazz musicians were able to participate in "jam sessions" at the Brubeck Institute at the University of the Pacific in Stockton, California. One delegate was on her seventh visit to the United States on behalf of the Open World Program, although it was only her first time in New Mexico. Perhaps if Congress continues funding the program, she'll be able to make another tour and hit all the states.

According to a 2004 report by the GAO, "Because the program does not have formalized strategic and performance plans with measurable indicators, it is difficult to determine the extent to which it is targeting and reaching the right people and giving them experiences that result in improved mutual understanding. While Open World does survey delegates about their experiences, it has not yet conducted a full program evaluation to determine progress toward its long-term goals. Open World officials agree that such an evaluation is necessary and hope to conduct one in the near future." Also, "it does not prepare financial statements that can be subject to an independent audit. In addition, Open World does not have an audit or financial management advisory committee to advise the Board of Trustees on financial management, accountability, and internal control issues. Finally, Open World is not disclosing the value of services contributed by U.S. volunteers who support the program—information that generally accepted accounting principles encourage entities to disclose."

Typically, the government has created multiple programs that accomplish the same task—the Russian Far East Program sends American businesses to expand Russia's presence in the global marketplace; the Open World Russian Leadership Program brings Russian politicians to the U.S. to learn about democracy to strengthen Russia's economy. CAGW has tracked $28 million in pork-barrel funds for the program to "train" 7,200 Russian leaders. The Open World Program has received $64.5 million since its inception, making the $30 million in appropriations 46.5 percent of total U.S. funding for the program.

$5 Million for the Irish Peace Process Cultural Training Program

In the fiscal year 2000 Foreign Operations Appropriations Act, this one-time earmark was added in conference by House appropriator James Walsh (R-N.Y.) for the Irish Peace Process Cultural Training Program. As many as 4,000 young people from Northern Ireland were to enter the U.S. each year until 2002 and to work here for as long as three years. Participants would be brought to the United States "for the purpose of developing job skills and conflict resolution abilities in a diverse, peaceful, and prosperous environment" and will then "return home better able to contribute toward economic regeneration and the Irish peace process." It may be cheaper than the IFI, but it's still more than a wee bit "o" pork.

$250,000 for the International Law Institute at Georgetown University

These funds are going to continue the institute's training and support of lawyers and judges in the Commonwealth of Independent States. The $250,000 is equal to two years' salary for the 70 percent of graduating law students who chose to work in the private sector. (The breakdown equals $435 per student— tuition is $30,940 annually for the 575 students enrolled.)

$2 Million for Western Kentucky University's (WKU) 833 Print and Broadcast Journalism Students

The project, supported by Senate Foreign Operations Appropriations Subcommittee Chairman Mitch McConnell (R-Ky.), will give the students hands-on field training in foreign countries. It will also enable overseas broadcasters and journalists the chance to study in Bowling Green at WKU. The Senate Appropriations Committee wrote that it was "concerned about the success and sustainability of independent, non–state-controlled media" but that didn't stop Congress from throwing the money to WKU anyway. Sen. McConnell defended the funding, stating that "(WKU) has one of the top journalism programs in the United States. [The program] will allow the university to showcase its credentials worldwide."

Soon after the appropriations came through, WKU flew 10 Indonesian broadcasters over to the U.S. for three weeks of studying the First Amendment, ethics, and news gathering. Indonesia has been in the midst of constant upheaval, with news streaming in about armed uprisings, corruption, and economic crises. With the changing climate of Indonesia, it's no wonder Indonesians are willing to fly to America at taxpayers' expense for three weeks of journalism "training."

$400,000 for the Cochran Fellowship Program

The program was established by, and named for, Senate appropriator Thad Cochran (R-Miss.) in 1984. It is supposed to provide private U.S.-based, non-academic training that will acquaint Russian farmers with American agricultural practices. Let's hope that American farmers don't convince their Russian counterparts to become addicted to subsidies.

$8 Million for the U.S. Dairy Industry

In 2002, Congress skimmed $8 million from the taxpayers' wallets to help the U.S. dairy industry become more competitive by promoting U.S. technology, equipment, inputs, and industry-based technical assistance in developing markets.

Taxpayers already heavily support the U.S. dairy industry. The Milk Income Loss Contract is a $2 billion annual program that subsidizes farmers when the price of milk drops. It replaced the processor-funded Northeast Interstate Dairy Compact, which was eliminated after Midwest dairy states said it was unfair. In its first month, October 2003, MILC paid out nearly $500 million, far above what was originally estimated. MILC expires in October 2005, but a group of legislators is pushing hard to extend the program for two more years.

The argument for assistance for the U.S. dairy industry is that dairy producers cannot compete under European regulations, and subsidies are needed in order to keep the industry stable and growing. However, the U.S. dairy industry is *moooo*ving along nicely, with annual sales value reaching $43 billion ($21 billion in fluid milk manufacturing such as milk, sour cream, and dairy substitutes; and $22 billion in cheese products).

$10.6 Million for the International Arid Lands Consortium (IALC)

The IALC, created by Congress in 1990, has received $10.6 million since 1994 to continue research on water issues in the Middle East. The consortium, located in Tucson, falls in the district of then-House Foreign Operations Appropriations Subcommittee Chairman Jim Kolbe (R-Ariz.). An advocate of the earmark, Sen. Dick Durbin (D-Ill.), defends the appropriations for the consortium because he feels "the looming issue of water and energy in the Middle East" is an important factor for Americans. Perhaps the real reason Sen. Durbin protects the funding is because the University of Illinois is one of the eight universities that help decide which projects receive funding.

Defenders of the IALC funding argue that the research projects also help solve the water crises facing the U.S. But while Congress tries to quench the thirst in the Middle East, arid states such as Arizona and New Mexico face drought problems almost yearly.

$1 Million for the Conflict Transformation Across Cultures (CONTACT) Program at the School for International Training in Brattleboro, Vermont

The CONTACT program has four "world learning" centers. Headquartered in the state of Senate Foreign Operations Appropriations Subcommittee Member Patrick Leahy (D-Vt.), the School for International Training in Brattleboro received a one-time $1 million earmark in 2002. Through this program, CONTACT students "explore the causes and complexities of contemporary conflict, examining methods that respond to conflict without perpetuating cycles of revenge, hostility, and division" and "reflect on forgiveness and reconciliation in their own traditions . . . to heal the wounds of war." In the last five years, CONTACT has averaged 40 participants per year, making this appropriation a $25,000 subsidy for each student.

$500,000 for the International Coffee Organization (ICO)

ICO is an intergovernmental body composed of countries that import and export coffee, and, according to its Web site, "is committed to improving conditions in the world coffee economy." The U.S. joined ICO in 1963, but ceased to be a member in 1993, refusing to sign the International Accord and disagreeing with what the U.S. saw as ICO's attempt to control prices and the coffee market. Ten years later, Congress added $500,000 in conference for ICO.

This effort was supposed to be an answer to the plummeting world coffee market in 2002. Due to the increase in producing cheaper-quality coffee, the coffee industry experienced a dramatic drop in revenue, which had a devastating affect on Latin American coffee farmers. In response, international and U.S. groups pressured the State Department to rejoin the ICO, which would help stabilize the international coffee market.

Pablo Dubois of ICO stated that "the United States is very important for the balance of world coffee consumption" because the country may provide "financial resources for coffee development projects." Robert Nelson from the National Coffee Association in the United States said in a statement that the U.S. decision was historic: "U.S. membership, through taking an active leadership role, can very much ensure future sustainability of the worldwide coffee industry."

The U.S. has recently announced that it will rejoin ICO, and the $500,000 appropriated for the organization in 2003 may act as the down payment. It seems the coffee industry just can't survive without the help of the U.S. A popular drink worldwide, the coffee industry rakes in about $70 billion in retail sales annually. And Starbucks just raised its prices!

Interior:
National Pork Service

The Department of Interior has had its fair share of problems in the past. From a grossly mismanaged Bureau of Indian Affairs to a National Park Service (a.k.a. National Pork Service) that has a $4.9 billion backlog of maintenance projects, one would think that appropriators would take extra care of America's most precious natural resource: tax dollars.

$25.2 Million for "America's Industrial Heritage"

The Southwestern Pennsylvania Heritage Preservation Commission's "America's Industrial Heritage" is a theme park covering nine industrial sites in southwestern Pennsylvania, courtesy of Rep. John Murtha (D-Pa.). In 1993, a Government Accountability Office (GAO) report found the scope of the project undefined. The rationale to start the commission was because of Pennsylvania's struggling economy during the 1980s. Twenty years later, Pennsylvania is still struggling and the commission has been of very little help.

$2 Million for an Ancient Canoe in Hawaii

In 1991, Sen. Daniel Inouye (D-Hawaii) and Sen. Daniel Akaka (D-Hawaii) secured $2 million for the Native Hawaii Culture and Arts Program to construct and sail an ancient canoe that depicted what native Hawaiians had to do to migrate.

How does a Senator get Congress to appropriate $2 million for a canoe? The canoe, which is a replica of a Polynesian canoe, now stands 57 feet and weighs 17 thousand pounds. The goal was to show how the first Hawaiians sailed to their new home, which, incidentally, had been successfully reenacted in 1976. Donald Duckworth of the Bishop Museum, where the canoe is on display, has nothing but praise for Inouye, commenting to the press, "Certainly out here, we admire and respect Senator Inouye's translation of our needs."

Sen. John McCain (R-Ariz.) says this boondoggle slipped by him. He noted lawmakers slip requests for special projects into huge appropriations bills that no one is likely to scrutinize. (For example: Inouye managed to use a 203-page military-appropriations bill to get a company a 30-year monopoly on the inter-island cruise business in Hawaii. "You give one company a monopoly to cruise the very beautiful islands of Hawaii, the consumers are going to pay, and clearly, far in excess of what they otherwise would if there was competition," said Sen. McCain.)

$27 Million for the Steamtown National Historic Site in Scranton, Pennsylvania

Defenders of the project call Steamtown an important tribute to steam locomotion. Conversely, the project has also been called an "inconsequential, third-rate collection in a place that has no relevance" by a former curator of the Smithsonian Museum. CAGW has tracked $27 million in appropriations since 1991 for this project, but federal appropriations for Steamtown total $66 million. According to a 2004 news report, "When Steamtown National Historic Site in Scranton opened in 1995, the National Park Service estimated the site would attract 400,000 visitors each year. Instead, attendance in 2003 was 117,994." That is more than 70 percent less than advertised. But at least the locals are utilizing Steamtown. Apparently, the "skater crowd" of Scranton assembles at the Mall at Steamtown, and has become such a problem that the local police are cracking down on the misbehaving skateboarders and roller-bladers. The project has had some lasting impact, demonstrating the clout of former Rep. Joe McDade (R-Pa.).

$2 Million for Walk on the Mountain

Visitors to this covered skywalk in downtown Tacoma, Washington, will be able to see Mt. Rainier National Park in the distance, but only on one of the 57 clear days a year in Tacoma. The cost per viewing day for one year is $35,088, thanks to House appropriator Norm Dicks (D-Wash.).

$30.4 Million for the FDR Memorial in Washington, D.C.

President Franklin D. Roosevelt once said the only memorial he wanted was a monument no larger than his desk. He must be rolling over in his grave right now. He got 9 acres.

Established in 1955, the FDR Commission was charged with building a memorial for our thirty-second president. The commission decided to ignore FDR's desire for a small memorial, which already existed behind the U.S. Archives building. Instead, the commission planned, and Congress authorized, a $47 million, 9-acre garden plaza in downtown Washington. Taxpayers provided $27 million for construction of the new memorial. Controversy over design and architectural plans kept construction in limbo until September 1991, when ground was finally broken.

Ironically, the project was supposed to be privately funded. In fiscal year 1997, $375,000 was added by the Senate for a memorial dedication ceremony, and in fiscal year 2000, $3 million was added in conference for expansion of the new FDR Memorial. The House Committee stated that it was "shocked" to see a budget request to expand the memorial and reminded the National Park Service (who was tasked with renovating the memorial) that private fundraising efforts fell short of projections. The committee also said that expansion of the memorial would not be done at taxpayer expense. Nevertheless, the $3 million for the expansion went through.

$3.4 Million for Building Rehabilitation at the National Center for Preservation Technology in Louisiana

The center was scheduled to be built in Georgia, but when Sen. Wyche Fowler (D-Ga.) lost his Senate seat, Senate appropriator J. Bennett Johnston (D-La.) had the project moved to Natchitoches College, which, at that time, had not a single employee experienced in preservation study.

$100,000 for the Alaska Gold Rush Centennial Task Force and $100,000 for the Alaska Gold Rush Centennial Exhibits and Living History Presentations

According to Alaska's Department of History and Archaeology's Web site, "The Alaska State Legislature designated 1994–2004 the Alaska Gold Rush Centennial Decade. The Office of History and Archaeology has promoted the 100th anniversaries of gold discoveries that took place around Alaska and coordinated the state's commemoration programs." One of the projects undertaken by the Centennial Task Force to promote Alaskan tourism was an online treasure hunt. According to a task force press release, "The winner received a 12-day Gold Rush cruise and land tour for two aboard Holland America Line's luxury Noordam, complete with first-class tickets on Delta Air Lines." The gold in dem dar hills is federal tax dollars.

$300,000 for the Accokeek Foundation

In 1999, House appropriator Steny Hoyer (D-Md.) grabbed $300,000 for the Accokeek Foundation. The Accokeek Foundation is a nonprofit group established to preserve the land directly across the water from George Washington's Mt. Vernon. In fiscal year 2003, it had 186,000 visitors. With a $2 fee for adults and $5 for families, they could have paid for the $300,000 by increasing the cost for visitors. Looks like "Washington Crossing the Delaware" means dollars bills are floating toward Maryland's shoreline.

$3.6 Million for the National First Ladies Library

The site of this library is a former bar and brothel. In 1999, news reports indicated that House Interior Appropriations Subcommittee Chairman Ralph Regula (R-Ohio) slipped $300,000 of the $2.8 million appropriated that year into the National Park Service budget in an attempt to get the library designated as a national park. According to a 2002 article, "One of the tour guides is a man who impersonates 10 first ladies for performance, at a low price ('I can't make much or it would negate my Social Security'), purely out of love of history, he says, and also women like Mary Todd Lincoln, Florence Harding and Helen Taft. He's given up being Eleanor Roosevelt—no longer able to maintain her high falsetto voice."

The question remains as to why Ohio is housing this library. The project was the brainchild of the wife of Rep. Regula. Mystery solved.

$700,000 for the Saturn V Rocket at the U.S. Space and Rocket Center in Huntsville, Alabama

House Interior Appropriations Subcommittee Member Robert Cramer (D-Ala.) nabbed $700,000 for the Saturn V Rocket at the U.S. Space and Rocket Center in his district in Huntsville, Alabama. A private investor offered $101 million to purchase the Space Center with the guarantee to assume $15–$18 million worth of debt and invest up to $10 million in maintenance and improving exhibits. The state is reluctant to sell because it is one of Alabama's most popular tourist attractions. However, it is not a money-wasting facility, unless one counts the subsidy provided by non-visitors.

$176,000 for the Reindeer Herders Association in Alaska

The Reindeer Herders Association, in cooperation with the Bureau of Indian Affairs, is dedicated to improving the health and economic value of Alaska's reindeer herds. In 1999, Alaska's reindeer meat sales totaled $295,000. The appropriation to the Reindeer Herders Association counted for nearly 60 percent of their total meat sales, thanks to Senate Appropriations Committee Chairman Ted Stevens (R-Alaska).

$3.5 Million for the Vulcan Monument in Birmingham, Alabama

This 60-ton statue was created by New York sculptor Giuseppe Moretti in 1903 to represent Alabama at the 1904 World's Fair in St. Louis. After the World's Fair, it was moved back to Birmingham as a tribute to the steel industry. The city had an aggressive local fundraising campaign to refurbish the statue of Vulcan, the Roman God of Fire, but still needed to rely on federal funds to complete the project. Senate appropriator Richard Shelby (R-Ala.) forged ahead in this quest and procured $3.5 million worth of pork for the project. One hundred years later, it should not be the taxpayers' burden to restore the statue to its former glory days.

$425,000 for the George Ohr Arts and Cultural Center in Biloxi, Mississippi

The cultural center has been renamed to the Ohr-O'Keefe Museum, in honor of the late Biloxi potter George Ohr and former Biloxi Mayor Jeremiah O'Keefe. The museum is scheduled to open in January 2006 and is projected to cost $25 million. The Ohr-O'Keefe Museum, a Smithsonian affiliate, will highlight the eccentric nineteenth-century "Mad Potter of Biloxi," making it the first museum ever to be dedicated to a single potter. George Ohr predicted that "when I am gone, my work will be praised, honored, and cherished." It looks like Congress will help his prediction come true.

$1 Million for a DNA Study of Bears in Montana

In 2003, then-Senate Interior Appropriations Subcommittee Ranking Member Conrad Burns (R-Mont.) nabbed $1 million for a DNA study of bears in his home state. In response to this funding, Sen. John McCain (R-Ariz.) ridiculed this project during debate on the Senate floor: "One can only imagine and conjure up an idea as to how this might be used. Approach a bear: 'That bear cub over there claims that you're his father, and we need to take your DNA.' Approach another bear: 'Two hikers had their food stolen by a bear, and we think it is you. We have to get the DNA. The DNA doesn't fit, you [have] to acquit.'"

$275,000 for the Walking Box Ranch

The ranch, located in the state of Senate Interior Appropriations Subcommittee Member Harry Reid (D-Nev.), was originally founded in 1931 by B-movie actor Rex Bell. The site was visited by stars such as Clark Gable, Carole Lombard, Errol Flynn, Norma Shearer, and Lionel Barrymore. According to the *Las Vegas Review Journal* in December 2000, "Las Vegas' Gaming Investments paid $950,000 for the 38.5-acre ranch with historical ties to Hollywood's golden era, ending a month of negotiations between seller Viceroy Gold Corp. and several interested potential buyers." If the buyers had just won a few chips, maybe the taxpayer subsidy could have been avoided. Instead, Sen. Reid took a big gamble with taxpayers' money.

Labor, Health and Human Services, and Education: The Working Man's Pork

This ubiquitous appropriation funds everything from job training and museums to the National Institutes of Health. With such a large range of funding areas it is no surprise that Congress has found ample opportunity to fund its own pet projects. That means Congress is ignoring the real needs of the country and is instead funding unnecessary projects. The next time members of Congress complain about budgetary shortfalls, remind them that they spent $100,000 for the Tiger Woods Foundation.

$4 Million for the Dwight D. Eisenhower Leadership Program

In fiscal year 1994, $4 million was appropriated for the Dwight D. Eisenhower Leadership Program. The curriculum was designed to award grants of $175,000 to "stimulate and support the development of leadership skills among new generations of American college students." This program was created by Senate appropriator Arlen Specter (R-Pa.) and House Education and Labor Committee Ranking Member William Goodling (R-Pa.).

The program has received grant proposals ranging from hiring *Chillin' Time,* a Texas rap group, for "Rap and Eat" encounter sessions with "at-risk fifth graders," to funding a TV variety show entitled "The Spirit of Leadership" at the University of Arizona. A House report stated it bluntly: "The Administration has stated the activities supported by this program are part of many higher education institutions' curriculum, and therefore the program is a low priority for Federal funding." The Senate could have shown some leadership by zeroing out this project.

$3 Million for the Palmer Chiropractic School in Iowa and Florida

The Senate earmarked the first $1 million in 1994 for the Palmer Chiropractic School in Davenport in the state of Senate appropriator Tom Harkin (D-Iowa) to conduct chiropractic demonstrations. But the back-breaking funding doesn't stop there. The following year, the Senate provided a $936,000 grant to the school, and in 2004, $400,000 was added in conference for its sister school in Port Orange, Florida. In total, taxpayers have paid $2.936 million for research, equipment, and other needs at the Palmer Chiropractic School in Iowa and Florida.

The 1,797 students at the Davenport school are able to enjoy using the largest chiropractic college library in the world, and have exceptional equipment and facilities for their studies. The

Palmer school also offers a study abroad program for students interested in developing their techniques in countries such as Fiji, Haiti, and Nepal.

As Rush Limbaugh joked, "Who better to pay for back-cracking than the taxpayer?"

$103.8 Million for Consumer and Homemaking Education

From 1993 to 1995, $103.8 million was added for consumer and homemaking education. According to testimony by former Assistant Secretary for Vocational and Adult Education Betsy Brand, "The States currently have active, well-established consumer and homemaking programs. Nationally, States and localities spend almost $20 for every Federal dollar provided for this activity. Given the existing level of state and local support for consumer and homemaking education, we believe this activity would continue at the local level without direct Federal support." Fortunately, the president's fiscal year 1996 budget eliminated funding for this program.

$21.1 Million for Cooperative Higher Education

Cooperative education is the combination of classroom studies and on-the-job training, allowing students the chance to put their education to the test in the "real world." In fiscal year 1995, the Senate tucked in $6.9 million for cooperative education. According to the House report, "The Administration contends that cooperative education has been widely adopted among higher education institutions, often without Federal financial assistance, and therefore Federal support to promote this concept is no longer necessary."

The president's fiscal year 1996 budget eliminated funding for this program, but that didn't stop appropriators from handing out money for projects in their home states. In fiscal year 1998, $180,000 was added by the Senate in the state of Senate appropriator Byron Dorgan (D-N.D.) for North Dakota State University to expand cooperative education "beyond the traditional focus of placing students in business settings." The next year, the Senate added $250,000 in the state of Senate appropriator Richard Durbin (D-Ill.) for the Center for Urban Research and Learning at Loyola University of Chicago to conduct a cooperative higher education demonstration project. Congress certainly doesn't need any lessons in bipartisan cooperation in pork-barrel spending.

$1.9 Million for Historical Projects in Pennsylvania

In fiscal year 1998, Senate appropriator Arlen Specter (R-Pa.) grabbed $1.9 million for historical projects in Pennsylvania. The College of Physicians in Philadelphia received $1.1 million to maintain and interpret a historical collection of notes at the medical library. The college is a nonprofit educational institution that examines "the medical sciences and their place in society in order to enhance the understanding of medicine and the roles of physicians in history and in contemporary life." The college's historical library has a vast collection of manuscripts, books, and other resources open to the public at no charge. In 2002, the library became a historical medical library that no longer collects professional clinical and biomedical literature published after 1990.

While the documents have historical significance, the College of Physicians could have paid for the research project using the fees it collects for renting out its facilities for private events, including wedding receptions, corporate meetings, and bar/bat mitzvahs.

Pennsylvania is home to numerous coal mining sites and centers. Tourists wanting to check out Pennsylvania's mining history can visit the Coal Miners Memorial Museum in St. Michaels or the Coalport Area Coal Museum in McIntyre, which features displays on everyday life in a coal mining town in the early twentieth century. Yet, Sen. Specter decided that there just weren't enough coal mining exhibits in Pennsylvania. The mining library, which received an $800,000 earmark, was described as a "one-of-a-kind historical library in Pennsylvania's anthracite coal region to assist in the cataloging and historic preservation of detailed information regarding miners' compensation and occupational records, geological studies, maps, newspaper clippings, and more than 8,000 photographs." Sounds like something that should have been included in Steamtown or "America's Industrial Heritage" (see Interior) or not spent at all.

$75 Million for the Teacher Training in Technology Program

This earmark was added in conference in fiscal year 1999 to help ensure that all new teachers can teach effectively with technology. The House Appropriations Committee was against the funding, and to support its stance, cited a 1995 GAO report indicating that there were already 86 teacher training programs that trained more than a million teachers. The committee was unwilling to recommend increased funding or add confusion to the existing system of fragmented, overlapping, and duplicative teacher training programs.

The program, "Preparing Tomorrow's Teachers to Use Technology," gives out grants to various K–12 schools and higher education institutions to continue to improve teachers' and students' use of technology. Despite the millions of dollars poured into teacher training for technology, little progress has been made. In 2002, the Industrial College of the Armed Forces released a report that stated that "to truly transform educational delivery, technology must be available, mobile, flexible, intuitive, reliable, user-friendly, seamless, and nearly invisible. Arguably, today's educational technology satisfies none of these criteria. . . . Although computers and related information technologies were introduced to educators as educational tools more than three decades ago, one can find little evidence that these enabling technologies have materially altered the classroom. . . . Teachers [are not] effectively utilizing available technology to achieve high standards. Most have not changed the way they teach despite Internet access, nor are they under pressure to do so."

$10.7 Million for Internet Resources for Schools

While providing $75 million in appropriations funds to get teachers hooked up to modern technology, Congress has also provided generous support for classroom access to the Internet, interactive communications projects, and many other programs using today's modern technology. From Alaska to Montana to Maryland, appropriators have made sure that schools in their home states get a little extra cash for Internet projects.

States don't need appropriations for Internet resources. The 1996 Telecommunications Act allowed the FCC to impose a Universal Service Tax to provide "discount telecommunications services" to schools, libraries, and rural health facilities. The FCC charges long-distance providers, who pass on the costs to consumers in the form of higher telephone bills.

Since 1995, CAGW has tracked $10.675 million for Internet education pork-barrel projects. Some of the examples include:

🐖 A 1998 earmark for $1 million for a demonstration project to "provide interactive communications via the Internet to the information resources available between universities and their satellite campuses, community and public colleges, school and special libraries, and other entities" in the home state of Senate appropriator Conrad Burns (R-Mont.). The Senate report stated that it "urges" the money be sent to the Montana Information Consortium, which includes the University of Montana and Montana State University;

🐖 In 1999, Senate Appropriations Committee Chairman Ted

Stevens (R-Alaska) grabbed $850,000 for the Department of Education to develop an Internet-based curriculum and to provide training to teachers in Alaskan villages;

🐷 Senate appropriator Barbara Mikulski (D-Md.) was able to secure $1.5 million in 2002 for the Baltimore City Public School System to complete wiring the city's schools to the Internet; and

🐷 In fiscal years 2003 and 2004 $100,000 and $50,000 were added in conference, respectively, for the "Imagination Station" program at the Today Foundation in Dallas, Texas. The program was designed to deliver reading curriculum over the Internet using animation for "at-risk youth."

$34 Million for Ready to Learn Television

This program, which received earmarks in fiscal years 1998–2000, was designed to develop and distribute educational videos for preschool and elementary school children and their parents. The program is a collaboration between the Department of Education and the Corporation for Public Broadcasting (CPB). One of the new services provided through the Ready to Learn Television program is an expansion of "First Book," a program that provides more than 1 million books to disadvantaged children. The Ready to Learn initiative also provides free quarterly publications for parents with suggestions on how to "enhance the learning of preschool and early elementary school-aged children after the TV is turned off."

In fiscal year 1999, the House Appropriations Committee

argued that this activity could be carried out by CPB with the federal payments it already receives. In its 2003 Semiannual Report (March 31, 2003), the corporation stated that "CPB receives nearly all of its funding from Congress. . . . Appropriations for fiscal year 2003 are $365 million. Additionally, CPB receives grants from foundations or other organizations for specific projects. CPB must distribute at least 95 percent of its Federal appropriation to television and radio stations, producers of programs, or educational services." In addition, the privately owned and operated Channel One already provides educational programming and videos to 12,000 schools and is viewed by 8 million school children daily—at no cost to taxpayers.

$5 Million for a Telecommunications Demonstration Project for Mathematics

The budget justification submitted by the Department of Education indicated that "the program's single objective is to promote excellent teaching in mathematics through sustained professional development and teacher networks." Yet the program's measures of success, as outlined by the department, would be "the numbers of teachers trained, the estimated number of students taught by trained teachers, and the fact that teachers thought the program better than other professional development programs." The House Appropriations Committee was unwilling to recommend funding for a program with no specific, measurable output standards, but the Senate Appropriations

Committee had no reservation about adding another pork-barrel project to the bill.

$1.5 Million for the Touro Law Center in Central Islip, New York

Added in conference in 1999, this earmark was to be used by the Touro Law Center for the use of technology to bridge the gap between legal education and the actual practice of law. You do the math. At the time of the appropriation, there were 750 students at the law center. The government could buy $200 television sets for each one of them and require them to watch *Court TV, Law and Order,* and reruns of *Ally McBeal.* Less cost, more fun, and $1.3 million left over to refund to the taxpayers.

$43.5 Million for the National Constitution Center in Philadelphia, Pennsylvania

As part of a $24.4 million Labor/HHS Appropriations Pennsylvania package in 2000, Senate Labor/HHS Appropriations Subcommittee Chairman Arlen Specter (R-Pa.) and House appropriator John Murtha (D-Pa.) included $10 million for the National Constitution Center (NCC). The center also received $10 million in the Interior Appropriations Act that same year. The Senate Appropriations Committee agreed to spend the money in 2000, with the understanding that the NCC would be entirely self-sustaining and that no National Park Service funds would ever be required for operation of the facility. Silly Senate Committee, they should have realized that one appropriation would never whet the appetite of the Pennsylvania porkers. Five million dollars was added in fiscal year 2003 for the center. The total appropriations for this pork-barrel project amount to more than $43.5 million.

The center is a nonprofit, nonpartisan organization dedicated to "increasing public understanding of, and appreciation for, the Constitution, its history, and its contemporary relevance, through an interactive, interpretive facility within Independence National Historical Park and a program of national outreach, so that We the People may better secure the Blessings of Liberty to ourselves and our Posterity." Some posterity.

Although the NCC was created in 1988, groundbreaking for the center didn't commence until September 17, 2000—213 years to the day the U.S. Constitution was signed. President Bill Clinton presided over the ceremonies, which included the announcement of a $10 million gift from the Annenberg Foundation. The center named its interactive outreach wing the "Annenberg Center for Education and Outreach," in honor of the gift. Where's the wing named after taxpayers, since we all "donated" more than $43.5 million for the center?

$2.2 Million for the Los Angeles County Museum of Natural History

The Natural History Museum in Los Angeles has collected $2.225 million for construction, renovations, and other pork-barrel projects. For example, in fiscal year 2000, House appropriator Julian Dixon (D-Calif.) added $1 million in conference for the "Discovering the Tiniest Giants" exhibit at the Los Angeles County Museum of Natural History. The exhibit featured newly discovered dinosaur eggs from Argentina and, in the theme of "you can do it," encouraged children to imagine themselves as scientists involved in the Patagonia expedition and the laboratory work that followed. Can the children imagine themselves as the inheritors of a $7.5 trillion debt?

$594.2 Million for the Construction and Renovation of "Health Care and Other Facilities"

In the fiscal year 2001 Labor/HHS Appropriations Act, $226,224,000 was earmarked for these vague projects. The House did not request any funding, whereas the Senate requested only $10 million. In conference, appropriators not only tacked on an additional $216,224,000 to the Senate request, but they also compiled a list of health care facilities that would each receive a piece of this pork pie. There were no specific allocations in this list, but of the 208 health care facilities included, 119 were in states that have an appropriator on either the House or Senate

Labor/HHS Appropriations Subcommittee. That means that 7 percent of Congress (the 30 House and Senate Labor/HHS Sub-committee members) represented more than 57 percent of the facilities on this list.

It was déjà vu in 2002: $311,978,000 was added in conference for the construction and renovation of "health care and other facilities." The House and the administration requested no funding, while the Senate again requested $10 million. Of the 357 facilities cited, 229 were in states that have an appropriator on either the House or Senate Labor/HHS Appropriations Sub-committee. This time, 6 percent of Congress (the 32 House and Senate Labor/HHS subcommittee members) represented 64 percent of the facilities on the list. That's hazardous to the tax-payers' health.

$3.25 Million for the GRAMMY Foundation in Santa Monica, California

The foundation received funding for music education programs in schools across America. The GRAMMY Foundation partners with The Recording Academy, which puts together the annual Grammy Awards, a large production flashed during prime time television to honor the year's most outstanding musical artists. Presenters and performers at the 46th Annual Grammy Awards in 2004 received all sorts of goodies and trinkets in their $25,000–$27,000 gift baskets. Some of the freebies included Apple iPods, unique bracelets worth $1,000 each, lingerie, top-of-the-line blenders, gym memberships, and numerous gift certificates. Companies line up to give away their products, in the hope that celebrities will become regular customers.

$1.4 Million for the American Film Institute

Gross box office receipts in North America topped $10 billion in 2003. The movie business is surely the last U.S. industry that needs help from appropriators. And if the institute can't pay for education programs, how about asking some famous movie stars to pitch in? What about movie star and producer Drew Barrymore, who reportedly gets $14 million for each movie? Or, how about politically-minded Ben Affleck, who pulls in $17.5 million per film? Maybe he could promote his latest flop while educating the creative young minds of the future.

$273,400 for the Blue Springs Youth Outreach Unit to Combat Goth Culture in Blue Springs, Missouri

This wacky earmark was added in conference for educational training to combat goth culture in the state of Senate appropriator Christopher "Kit" Bond (R-Mo.). But it turns out that $132,000 of the cash was returned because officials apparently didn't need it. Rep. Sam Graves (R-Mo.) had requested the funds to study goth culture in Blue Springs. "It's one of those priorities that my constituents asked me to fight for," Graves explained at the time.

Some editorials suggested the federal government could save a lot of money by simply buying goth kids bright clothes and happy music. But others took the subject matter just a little too seriously. "It is my hope that this funding will give the officers in the Youth Outreach Unit the tools they need to identify goth culture leaders that are preying on our kids," Graves stated in a press release. Blue Springs Youth Outreach Unit officer Colby Lalli told the press, "It's not just the clothes they wear. We're seeing kids on the unit, whether it be suicide or homicide, they're just one more culture in our community that is at big risk, and we need to deal with that." "About 35 students have been identified with the goth culture," a Graves spokesman told the *Ledger-Enquirer* newspaper in Columbus, Georgia. "They're doing self-mutilation, animal sacrifices, the sort of violent behavior and drug use that possibly could lead up to what happened at Columbine in 1999 with Dylan Klebold and Eric Harris."

But then a funny thing happened. Blue Springs Youth Outreach Unit staffers finally admitted that many of the claims they made in their grant proposal were unfounded, so the remaining funds have been returned to the federal government.

$1.45 Million for Teaching Jazz History at the University of Idaho

The University of Idaho, located in the state of Senate Labor/HHS Appropriations Subcommittee Member Larry Craig (R-Idaho), received the funding to preserve the history of jazz and teach it to future generations. The university is certainly preserving one thing—the taxpayer blues.

$28.4 Million for the Iowa Communications Network

The Iowa Communications Network (ICN), located in Johnstown, Iowa, is a state agency that oversees a statewide fiber optics network for hospitals, public defense armories, libraries, schools, and other Iowan facilities. According to its Web site, the network "brings additional dollars into the state because of its uniqueness as an infrastructure. During the period of 1992 through 2003, the Federal Government will have invested $155.6 million in projects to use the ICN infrastructure as a test bed. Averaged over the 12-year period of the ICN's existence, this amounts to an annual investment of $12.9 million." Taxpayers, phone home—your money is missing.

$3.8 Million for Halls of Fame

Here are a few "in conference" decisions that we prefer to call the "Hall of Shame" for Congress. Why do taxpayers have to foot a bill for "Hall of Fame" museums that attract millions of dues-paying visitors? A few of the halls of fame receiving appropriations funds include:

🐗 $1,119,000 for the National Baseball Hall of Fame in Cooperstown, New York. With five New York representatives on the House appropriations Committee (House Labor/HHS Appropriations Subcommittee Member Nita M. Lowey [D], and House Appropriators James Walsh [R], John Sweeney [R], Jose E. Serrano [D], and Maurice D. Hinchey [R]), Cooperstown could soon have a special wing for those that went to bat for this pork;

🐗 $900,000 for the National Aviation Hall of Fame in Dayton, Ohio, in the state of House appropriator Marcy Kaptur (D) and Senate appropriator Mike DeWine (R). The Hall of Fame has various levels of contribution amounts, from a youth membership fee of $25.00 to a corporate fee of $1,600;

🐗 $750,000 for the Rock and Roll Hall of Fame in Cleveland, Ohio, for the Rockin' the Schools Education Program. The program benefits students at Northeast Ohio schools and charges a minimal fee. Ohio should pay for its own educational outreach programs, not national taxpayers. It would be cheaper just to send each class a copy of the movie *School of Rock*; and

🐗 $90,000 for the National Cowgirl Museum and Hall of Fame in Fort Worth, Texas. In 2002, the museum relocated to a new, $21 million, 33,000 square foot building featuring three theaters, an expanded research library, a retail store, and a grand rotunda featuring Hall of Fame honorees.

$772,000 for Family Communications, Inc.

Family Communications, Inc. (FCI), headquartered in Pittsburgh, Pennsylvania, produced the *Mister Rogers' Neighborhood* children's television show for three decades. The nonprofit "seeks to support healthy emotional, social, and intellectual development at all ages." The organization has received appropriations for projects such as the National Preschool Anger Management Project and antiviolence programs. Why FCI collects appropriations when it already receives donations from private corporations, including the Heinz Endowments, the Ford Foundation, the Lilly Endowment, the Dyson Foundation, and the Sears-Roebuck Foundation, is anybody's guess.

$91.1 Million for Miscellaneous Pennsylvania Pork

In fiscal year 2004, 401 projects in Pennsylvania, or 21 percent of total Labor/HHS pork, were added in conference to the Labor/HHS Appropriations Act in the state of Senate Labor/HHS Appropriations Subcommittee Chairman Arlen Specter (R-Pa.), the districts of House Labor/HHS Appropriations Subcommittee Members John Peterson (R-Pa.) and Donald Sherwood (R-Pa.), and the districts of House appropriators John P. Murtha (D-Pa.) and Chaka Fattah (D-Pa.).

Among the projects are $20 million for the Pennsylvania Department of Education to help struggling schools; $6.8 million for 13 hospitals for "construction, renovation, and equipment";

$2,887,000 for 32 abstinence education programs; $950,000 for 14 arts programs; $725,000 for the Please Touch Museum in Philadelphia to develop educational programs focusing on hands-on learning experiences; $350,000 for the Allegheny Conference on Community Development in Pittsburgh, with Wars on Empire, Inc., for the 250th Anniversary of the French and Indian War Activities; $100,000 for the University of Pittsburgh Center for Sports Medicine to determine the prevalence of knee injuries in female athletes; $100,000 for Bradford High School to improve the metalworking program; $75,000 for East Stroudsburg University to preserve and develop exhibits for their Vintage Radio Programs and Jazz Museum; and $50,000 for the Saint Tikhon's Theological Seminary for the care and preservation of Russian artifacts.

The Pennsylvania porkers have grabbed $4.25 million for the Please Touch Museum in Philadelphia since fiscal year 2001. Fiscal hawk Rep. Jeff Flake (R-Ariz.) railed against the egregious pork items stuffed into the 2004 omnibus bill, and singled out the museum as an especially ridiculous pork-barrel project: "Doling out $725,000 to the Please Touch Museum seems appropriate for congressional appropriators who can't keep their hands off taxpayers' money."

$4.5 Million for the First Tee Program in St. Augustine, Florida

The group's mission is "to impact the lives of young people around the world by creating affordable and accessible golf facilities primarily to serve those who have not previously had exposure to the game and its positive values." In fiscal year 2004, a $1 million earmark was supposed to be used for "character education." This exemplifies what's wrong with pork-barrel spending.

The Office of Safe and Drug-Free Schools at the Department of Education provides competitive grants under the Partnerships in Character Education Project Program. Eligible entities include a state education agency in partnership with one or more local education agencies or local education agencies and nonprofit organizations, including institutions of higher education. The total budget for the program was $2,496,331 in fiscal year 2004. The average grant was projected to range from $100,000 to $550,000. The purpose of the program is to assist eligible entities "in designing and implementing character education programs that take into consideration the views of parents, students, students with disabilities . . . and other members of the community." Applications must meet the "absolute priority" or be able to integrate the character education program "into classroom instruction and to be consistent with State academic standards" and to carry out the program "in conjunction with other education reform efforts."

The First Tee Program's qualifications are clearly not up to par. Even worse, the earmark of $1 million is nearly twice the projected maximum for state education agencies. That means some qualified educational institution will not be getting the funds it may need because of the First Tee pork.

Since 1998, the Masters Tournament has given $7 million to the organization. Taxpayers are now even more "teed off" about wasteful spending.

Legislative:
Hogs on the Hill

This appropriation funds the day-to-day operations of Congress, including the Library of Congress. There have been years in which Congress showed restraint by not adding any pet projects. But, in other years, members of Congress succumbed to laying on the bacon.

$350,000 to Restore the House Beauty Salon

Congressional critics often say that politics isn't pretty. Members of Congress tried to change that by restoring the House beauty salon. As the saying goes, "Put a suit on a pig, it's still a pig."

$25,000 to Study the Location for a New House Staff Gymnasium

With numerous private health clubs in the metro D.C. area, including two within six blocks of the House office building, the study should have consisted of opening the Yellow Pages and finding the cheapest local gym.

$150,000 for the Library of Congress's Madison Building Security Funds

The conference report states that this fund appears to be ". . . duplicative of a combined House-Senate-Library of Congress effort for buildings and office access technology."

$11.6 Million for Joining Hands Across America

No, this is not the 1986 hunger and homeless fundraising event. The Library of Congress's Joining Hands Across America is a local community initiative that helps educators teach and utilize the Library's digital resources.

$4.8 Million for the U.S.-China Economic and Security Review Commission

This organization was established in October 2000 to monitor, investigate, and report to Congress on the national security implications of the bilateral economic relationship with the People's Republic of China. That would appear to duplicate the duties of the U.S. trade representative, the Departments of Commerce and State, and the numerous committees and subcommittees of the U.S. Congress.

$8.75 Million for Adventures of the American Mind

While its goal to incorporate the Library of Congress's digital collections into school curricula may sound reasonable, this money would be better spent rebuilding crumbling schools. Our tax dollars are a terrible thing to waste.

$629,000 for the Meeting of Frontiers

According to its Web site, "The project grew out of discussions in 1997–98 between members of Congress. . . . Nowhere was the new situation more apparent than in Alaska, where the end of the Cold war led to a revival of ethnic, religious, and economic ties going back to the Russian settlement of Alaska in the late eighteenth century." According to the 2000 Census Report, of the 579,740 people (over age 5) living in Alaska, only 2,952 (0.5 percent) speak Russian at home. The Cold War is over, but the war on the budget deficit has yet to begin.

$1.2 Million for the Abraham Lincoln Bicentennial Commission

The commission includes well-known pork-barrelers such as Senate appropriator Richard Durbin (D.Ill.) and House appropriator Ray LaHood (R-Ill.). The commission's Web site, *www. lincolnbicentennial.gov*, provides free posters of Abraham Lincoln. "Free" means at taxpayer expense.

Military Construction: When Porky Comes Marching Home

One of the Grace Commission's cornerstone recommendations was to establish a commission to review the closure and realignment of obsolete military facilities. Since 1988, there have been four Base Closure and Realignment Commissions (BRAC) that recommended closing 350 military facilities and realigning 145 others. To date, there have been 97 base closings, 55 major realignments, and more than $16 billion has been saved, with ongoing savings of $6 billion annually.

On top of appropriators' abuse of the budget process, in 1995, the Pentagon's inspector general deemed every military construction project to be suspect because justifications for them are very often "incomplete, poorly documented, or otherwise flawed." Funds taken from the military construction bills are being used to build golf courses, housing, and child development centers that should be funded by the morale, welfare, and recreation trust fund.

Despite the war on terror requiring every available dollar and the warnings of the inspector general, members of Congress have turned a deaf ear and inserted their own special interest projects into the Military Construction Appropriations bills, including efforts to protect their local facilities from the BRAC process.

$33 Million for the Bremerton Puget Sound Naval Shipyard in Washington

We don't need no stinkin' gym! Tell that to House appropriator Norm Dicks (D-Wash.), who secured $10.4 million in fiscal year 1996 for a physical fitness center at Bremerton Puget Sound Naval Shipyard. He ardently defended the project against the Porkbusters Coalition on the floor of the House and called the group's actions "a cynical attempt . . . to kill what is a legitimate program in an effort to gain some cheap, short-lived notoriety for being alleged budget cutters." At the time of that appropriation, there were five private gyms within a five-minute drive of the Bremerton Shipyard.

Besides the unnecessary physical fitness center, Rep. Dicks has secured appropriations for many other unauthorized projects at the Bremerton Naval Shipyard, including $13.3 million in fiscal year 1993 for bachelor enlisted quarters on the base, $4.3 million in fiscal year 1999 for a community support facility, and $1.93 million in fiscal year 2001 for a Navy fleet recreation facility. Since 1991, CAGW has tracked $33 million flowing into the shipyard.

$67.7 Million for Projects at Fort Indiantown Gap, Pennsylvania

Home to Pennsylvania's National Guard, near Harrisburg, the fort's Web site boasts that "with state of the art training facilities, we are always looking for ways to better serve our citizens-soldiers, as evidenced by the ongoing renovations of existing facilities as well as construction of new facilities." It seems taxpayers are also committed to providing the absolute best for the National Guard in Pennsylvania.

Fort Indiantown Gap has been on the base closing chopping block numerous times. Personnel reductions were made in the late 1990s, but each time, the facility has narrowly escaped from closing completely, thanks to the fort's champion, Senate appropriator Arlen Specter (R-Pa.). The senator has risen to defend the fort by nailing down $67.7 million in appropriations funds for projects, such as $4.58 million for a flight simulator and aeromedical complex in fiscal 1995; $9.8 million for training and barracks facilities in fiscal year 1996 (one of the years that the base was almost closed); and $8.5 million for phase I of a repair waste treatment plant and sewage line replacement project. In the future, taxpayers can expect to see millions more of their hard-earned dollars going down the drain for projects at Fort Indiantown Gap, thanks to Sen. Specter.

$114.1 Million for Unspecified Base Locations

In fiscal year 1997, the Senate added $17.9 million above the budget request for planning and design at unspecified world wide base locations. At the same time, the military was trying to reduce the number of bases overseas.

That wasn't the only time Congress appropriated funds for unspecified locations. Since 1991, a total of $114.1 million has been allotted for projects at worldwide unspecified locations. In 2004, the funding was "to address unplanned health or safety issues that may arise during Fiscal Year 2004" and "to satisfy critical and emergent mission requirements." Here's a critical issue: the $413 billion deficit.

$91.9 Million for the Grand Forks and Minot Air Force Bases in North Dakota

Senate appropriator Byron Dorgan (D-N.D.) has been instrumental in securing funding for the Air Force bases in Grand Forks and Minot. The bases have been able to spend the hard-earned dollars of taxpayers for "vital" projects, including new physical fitness centers, taxiway repairs, and family housing renovations. Since 1991, Minot Air Force Base has received $48.5 million in earmarks, and Grand Forks, $43.4 million.

Minot Air Force base has been mentioned more than once in the yearly announcements of possible base closings. But the base can continue to rely on Sen. Dorgan's generous support.

According to a 2004 article written by the editors of *Fargo-Grand Forks' Forum,* "Dorgan's record of getting a federal share for his state . . . is well-known and respected. Even North Dakotans who disagree with the positions he takes as a Democratic leader in Washington recognize his ability to put politics aside when going after necessary federal support for North Dakota." See, there are issues that transcend partisan politics.

$4.3 Million to Tear Down 19 Naval Radio Towers in Maryland

In 1999, Senate appropriator Barbara Mikulski (D-Md.) obtained $4.3 million to tear down 19 naval radio towers at Greenbury Point, Maryland. Originally, the towers were scheduled to be demolished starting in 2000 in order to preserve the "natural setting" of the rabbits and deer living in the 231-acre area known as Greenbury Point. At the time of the funding, the Naval Academy hadn't received permission to tear down some of the towers because the 80-year-old structures were designated historical sites.

While 16 of the 19 radio towers were torn down in December 1999, the three remaining towers were turned over to Maryland for "telecommunications or training purposes." The structures then became home to 19 osprey pairs. The Naval Academy took special care not to disrupt the birds and "provided new platforms [for the ospreys] before the towers were demolished." There are no reports on how many deer and rabbit lives the military was able to save.

$14 Million for the Arvin Cadet Physical Development Center in New York

The Senate added $14 million for the construction of the Arvin Cadet Physical Development Center at the U.S. Military Academy, West Point, New York, in fiscal year 2000. Although there was a budget request for this project, the House Committee concluded: "The Department of the Army estimates its current backlog of physical fitness centers to be $219 million. This backlog consists of 30 different projects at an average cost of $7.3 million. In spite of this backlog, the Army is in the midst of a three-phase, multi-year project to revitalize, by partial replacement, the Arvin Center. The total cost of this project is estimated at $85 million, more than 10 times the average cost for a physical fitness center." Thus, the House decided that funding should be deferred. The conferees capped total spending on the project at $63 million (only six times the average cost for a fitness center), citing a report that a proposed $17 million seismic upgrade (20 percent of the original cost) was neither cost-effective nor feasible. One hopes the military plans for national security contingencies on a more realistic basis. The last seismic disturbance in New York was in 1884.

$335.9 Million for Military Construction Projects in Mississippi

The appropriators from Mississippi have shipped hundreds of millions of taxpayer dollars to military construction projects in their home state. Since 1995, $78.4 million has been appropriated to the Air National Guard, Army Reserve, and Navy bases in Gulfport, Mississippi, alone. The total amount of military construction pork for Mississippi is $335.9 million since 1995.

In fiscal year 2000, Senate appropriator Thad Cochran (R-Miss.) and House Military Construction Appropriations Subcommittee Member Roger Wicker (R-Miss.) secured $45.1 million for a series of projects, including: $20.7 million for family housing at the Gulfport Naval Construction Battalion Center; $6.9 million for the warfighting center at the Stennis Space Center; and $1.4 million for channel dredging at Pascagoula Naval Station because Trent Lott's ship (see Defense) apparently needs a deeper channel.

In an October 1999 interview with *The Third Branch* (a newsletter of the federal courts), Sen. Cochran was asked about finding adequate funding for budget shortfalls. He said, "This budget process has turned into an exercise of political one-upsmanship for this Administration and this Congress. It is an unfortunate situation, and I think it has potential for real harm in the budget process if we continue to see the process deteriorate like we have in the last few years. Now you can lay blame wherever you choose, but I think this Administration has gotten to the point that they can't be trusted to keep their word on an agreement with respect to the budget process. There's absolutely no credibility left on matters of appropriations and spending priorities. It's a very unfortunate situation." Yes Senator, it is unfortunate . . . unfortunate, indeed.

$12.8 Million for Miramar Marine Corps Air Station in California

The base, located in the northern suburbs of San Diego, is located in the district of House appropriator Randy "Duke" Cunningham (R-Calif.). In fiscal year 2000, the House added $6.3 million for a physical fitness center at Miramar Marine Corps Air Station. Sources indicate that at the time of the appropriation, Miramar already had a gym with high-tech fitness equipment, including a Stairmaster with Internet access.

$38 Million for Projects in West Virginia

As in every other appropriations bill, Senate Appropriations Committee Ranking Member Robert Byrd (D-W.Va.) always makes sure to stuff the military construction bill with enough pork to sustain every nook and cranny of West Virginia. In fiscal years 2002 alone, Sen. Byrd added $38 million worth of projects, including $21.3 million for a center/organizational maintenance shop for the Army National Guard at Glen Jean; $6.4 million for a readiness center for the Army National Guard at Williamstown; $2 million for an integrated special operations facility at Camp Dawson; and $100,000 for a U.S. Army Museum Support Center in Martinsburg. There are at least nine major Army museums, and there are several subdivisions of museums.

The 2002 military construction appropriations gifts helped build the new Robert C. Byrd Regional Training Institute at

Camp Dawson to provide training for Active, National Guard, and Army Reserve units from the Eastern United States. Columnist Robert Novak described the new training institute as "the hub of the senator's plan to make his state the command center for anti-terrorist activities. That is only the most audacious instance of lawmakers turning the war against terrorism into a more lavish pork barrel."

$120.9 Million for McConnell Air Force Base in Wichita, Kansas

One of the many pork projects at McConnell Air Force Base in the district of House Military Construction Appropriations Subcommittee Member Todd Tiahrt (R-Kansas) was $5.1 million for a health and wellness center in fiscal year 2002. Improvements to the fitness center included renovating current workout areas and building a new gymnasium and group exercise areas.

McConnell is home to the largest midair refueling wing in the world. While many other bases have to worry about being included in the current round of base closures, Rep. Tiahrt has assured the base personnel that they need not to be concerned, thanks to former Sen. Robert Dole (R-Kansas). "I think Bob Dole had a lot to do with it. . . . He was majority leader and he was very influential, probably the most influential man in Washington, D.C. We dumped a lot of money into McConnell, and that made a difference." Hopefully, there's more to Bob Dole's legacy.

$56.5 Million for Fort Rucker, Alabama

Since 1991, Senate appropriator Richard C. Shelby (R-Ala.) has funneled $56.5 million in military construction projects to Fort Rucker. Some of the projects include $1.3 million for road upgrades in 1994; $1 million for the Cairns Army Air Field fire station in 2000; and $3.5 million for a physical fitness center for the Army at Fort Rucker in 2003. The senator was able to bring home $20.8 million worth of military construction projects to all facilities in Alabama for fiscal year 2003.

Sen. Shelby does his best to protect Fort Rucker and other Alabama bases from closures by shoveling millions in appropriations funds back to the state. In a 2004 *Northport Gazette* editorial, Sen. Shelby stated that "we must not forget the importance of our military bases to Alabama and the nation. Communities in and around Fort Rucker, Redstone Arsenal, Anniston Army Depot, Maxwell/Gunter Air Force Base, and Guard and Reserve facilities across the state expressed their concerns to me about the upcoming round of base closings. This is by far the largest round of base closings we have seen and every facility in the country will be considered. I am confident, however, that our bases are in a good position to survive this round of closings, and I am committed to providing them with the support they need to maintain their presence here in Alabama."

$119.8 Million for Eielson Air Force Base in Alaska

Senate Appropriations Committee Chairman Ted Stevens (R-Alaska) snatched $34 million for Alaskan military construction projects in 2004, including $15.8 million for a joint security forces complex at Eielson Air Force Base. The complex isn't the only project Sen. Stevens has procured for the base. Since 1996, CAGW has tracked $119.8 million worth of earmarks for Eielson Air Force Base for projects, including: $4 million for boiler rehabilitation in 1996; $6 million for a potable water storage upgrade in 1998; and $10.7 million for runway repairs in 2000.

$1.4 Million for a Dog Kennel at Elmendorf Air Force Base, Alaska

Another project included in the fiscal year 2004 Military Construction Appropriations Act was $1.4 million to replace a working dog kennel at Elmendorf Air Force Base. Money for a dog kennel in Alaska? Pork-buster Sen. John McCain (R-Ariz.) challenged the earmark during a Senate debate on the bill: "While some of our soldiers and sailors have been on food stamps, we have found a way to provide $1.4 million to replace a working dog kennel. . . . It is good to see that Fido has not been left out of this year's military construction appropriations." Senate appropriator Kay Bailey Hutchison (R-Texas) defended the expenditure, stating that "the kennel is for dogs at an Air Force base. . . . dogs in Alaska need a place to stay, too."

Transportation: Driving Miss Piggy

From the Wright Brothers' first flight in Kitty Hawk, North Carolina, to the first automobile rolling off the assembly line in Michigan, America has a rich history of transportation accomplishments. Today, transportation is essential in shuttling cargo and people from one destination to another. The federal government's role in providing safe roads is undeniable. But members of Congress are taking taxpayers for a ride when they appropriate money for transportation pork-barrel projects, meaning that no appropriations bill is safe.

Every time a family or business fills up its car or truck, a hefty 14 percent tax is placed on each gallon to fund local and national transportation projects. What most Americans don't know is that this money also goes to fund some absolutely ridiculous pork-barrel projects. The Transportation Appropriations Act is becoming more and more popular with politicians because transportation projects are one of the few earmarks that people can actually see. Politicians claim that building a road or a bridge, or funding local buses, shows that the government is truly working for the American public. But some projects first help fuel incumbents' campaigns. Truth be told, every project sneaked into the budget at the last minute represents a complete breakdown of the budgetary system and forces Congress to consider raising gas taxes even higher.

$10.2 Million for a Ramp and Reconstruction to Improve Access to a Privately Owned Stadium in Milwaukee

In 1991, if then-Sen. Bob Kasten (R-Wisc.) bet that bringing home the bacon to the tune of $10.2 million for a ramp and reconstruction to improve access to Milwaukee County Stadium would translate into votes from the diehard Milwaukee Brewer fans and return him to the Senate, then he was mistaken. He lost to Russ Feingold (D-Wisc.).

Nevertheless, one has to wonder about that $10.2 million, especially in light of the fact that in 1996, Milwaukee broke ground to build what would become the Brew crew's new $400 million home—Miller Park. Did taxpayers have to foot that bill? Consider this nugget: HBO's *Real Sports* reported that the Milwaukee Brewers were paying more than $2 million a year to owner Bud Selig, his daughter Wendy Selig-Prieb, and son-in-law Laurel Prieb during the 1990s, when the team was negotiating and receiving public subsidies for Miller Park. As for Milwaukee County stadium, the beneficiary of the $10.2 million appropriation in 1991, it was demolished on February 21, 2001. Green Bay East High School now stands on that site.

$1 Million for a Study of Bicycling and Walking Safety

Rep. Martin Sabo (D-Minn.) called for taxpayers to spend $1 million to "determine current levels of bicycling and walking and identify the reason why they are not better uses as a means of transportation." Here's a clue: There are no bike lanes, it's dangerous, there's no place to park, and finally, it's sweaty. In 1991, *Time* magazine scolded the congressman: "Sabo doesn't ride a bicycle. But his two daughters, who do, probably could tell him as much as a high-priced DOT study."

$55 Million for Corridor H Construction

Trying to find one transportation project in West Virginia to highlight is equivalent to trying to find one grain of sand in the middle of the desert. Sen. Robert Byrd (D-W.Va.) has been one of the most prolific pork-barrelers in the history of the Republic. To show his unabashed love of highway pork, the senator once quipped, "You might as well slap my wife as take highway money from West Virginia."

Back to Corridor H. To "stimulate economic growth in rural Appalachia," Congress passed the Appalachian Regional Development Act (ARDA) in 1965, creating the Appalachian Regional Commission (ARC) and authorizing the creation of the Appalachian Development Highway System (ADHS). That same year, the ARC designated Corridor H, among 23 projects, to be developed. However, because of its relatively high cost and low traffic volume, Corridor H, initially proposed as a two-lane parkway through West Virginia and into part of Virginia, was the last to be constructed.

In the late 1970s, a four-lane truck route was suggested on Corridor H, and although the Federal Highway Administration (FHWA) called it "overbuilt" and "excessive," construction on the road continued despite protests by environmental groups. According to the official Corridor H Web site, the project was put on hold in 1984 due to "funding issues."

"The project was revived in 1990 when Senator Robert C. Byrd (D-WV) chaired the Appropriations Committee and began funneling federal money to the Mountain State. Parts of the FBI, IRS and other agencies were moved to West Virginia, but the biggest single source of money available was the highway fund and therefore Byrd's biggest target. Supporting a Corridor H truck route were the expanding poultry industry, plus timber and real estate interests. Citizens supporting Corridor H expressed concerns about safety on some existing roads, and stated the belief that a four-lane would bring jobs or make commuting easier," according to an opposition group named Corridor H Alternatives (CHA).

There have been multiple lawsuits fighting against the construction of Corridor H. In 1996, CHA sued, alleging that "FHWA violated the National Environmental Protection Act (NEPA) by failing to consider an improved roadway alternative (IRA) and by failing to prepare a Supplemental EIS to consider impacts of the Corrick's Ford Battlefield alignment shift," according to the project's official Web site, *www.wvcorridorh.com*. Finally, the Web site notes, "WVDOT was ordered by the Court to halt construction of Corridor H except for the 3.5 mile section near Elkins." Even with multiple lawsuits, construction of Corridor H continues.

$3 Million for the Orlando Streetcar Project (OSCAR)

Orlando is most well-known for Disney World. But outside the hallowed walls of Mickey Mouse's home lies a rather "goofy" idea—the Orlando Streetcar Project (OSCAR). The plan called for a five-car, two-mile circular transit system with an estimated cost that would exceed $40 million if completed by 2010. At that time, a free shuttle bus service (FreeBee), carrying 1,700 riders per day, served the same route. Projections for ridership upon completion of OSCAR were 5,400. Here's an update to the "Streetcar Named Outrageous" project: No streetcar was ever built. Instead, the OSCAR project morphed into the LYMMO bus rapid transit (BRT) service project, a free downtown shuttle loop that uses natural gas and powered buses. A 2003 University of Florida study praised LYMMO by stating that the project:

🐷 improved bus speeds and schedule adherence;
🐷 increased ridership as a result of improved bus speeds, schedule adherence, and convenience;
🐷 minimized the effect of BRT on other traffic;
🐷 isolated the effect of each BRT feature on bus speed and other traffic; and
🐷 assessed the effect of BRT on land use and development.

But the study also put a disclaimer on its findings, noting that "during the evaluation process . . . historical and performance-related data were not always available and, when available, were not in sufficient detail. This data gap caused many of the tasks of the LYMMO BRT project evaluation to be more subjective than objective in nature than as originally scoped. While historical data related to the construction of the project was available, data was not systematically collected since service inception. The collection of such data would have allowed for before and after comparisons of the performance characteristics of the previous Downtown Orlando circulator (FreeBee) and the LYMMO BRT system. One valuable lesson learned from the LYMMO BRT evaluation is that (particularly as the FDOT and the Federal Transit Administration move forward with funding for the planning, construction, and operation of BRT systems) there is a critical need for data collection to begin immediately and systematically in order to allow for a detailed evaluation of the effectiveness of specific BRT components and the effectiveness of the overall BRT system." Or, just throw more money at LYMMO and ask questions later.

$9.7 Million for the Jacksonville Automated Skyway Express (ASE)

From the beginning, this project has epitomized the word "boondoggle." The projected cost is $34 million per mile. One Department of Transportation official said the ASE has gone from a serious transportation project in the late 1970s to nothing more than an expensive "amusement ride" today. *ABC-news.com* refers to the Skyway Express as the "Riderless Express," because almost no one rides it. Ridership statistics indicate about 3,000 daily riders after the federal government doled out $182 million, or $60,667 per passenger.

$5 Million for a High-speed Intercity Magnetic Levitation Project Between Philadelphia and Pittsburgh

The initial 47-mile project linking the Pittsburgh Airport to Pittsburgh and its eastern suburbs has been under study since 1990. According to congressional testimony, the project has two objectives: (1) to demonstrate the first high speed maglev project in the U.S. and (2) to establish the precision fabrication technology to implement maglev technology anywhere in the U.S. The rugged physical terrain, a full four-season climate, and stops at an airport, downtown, and in the suburbs would demonstrate the full potential of the technology in a variety of environments. The project is intended to be the first stage of a system that would eventually provide high-speed (300 mph) service west to Cleveland and east to Philadelphia. It is still in the early stages and far from being completed.

$1 Million for the Columbus Port-of-Entry Realignment in New Mexico

As one of the three points of entry from Mexico into New Mexico, Columbus has a large number of vehicles traveling its roads daily. The state government began expanding border marketing and infrastructure in order to attract more growth and development in Columbus. New billboards were constructed, facilities were renovated, and parking lots were expanded.

As part of the renovations, Senate Transportation Appropriations Subcommittee Member Pete Domenici (R-N.M.) asked for and received $1 million to realign the current port-of-entry facilities in Columbus. New Mexico Secretary of Transportation Pete Rahn tried unsuccessfully to stop the funding because he did not want the state to be liable for 25 percent of the cost of what he felt was an unnecessary project.

$132 Million for Alaska Railroad Rehabilitation

Sen. Ted Stevens (R-Alaska) is a master magician. He takes tax dollars and makes them disappear; eventually, they show up in Alaska. One of his finest sleight of hand tricks is his funding for Alaska Railroad Rehabilitation. A closer look at the Alaska Railroad project indicates that Sen. Stevens is no David Copperfield because the project has been a complete failure. It's like throwing money into an open pit. The railroad extends 498 miles from Seward through Anchorage, the largest city in Alaska, to the city of Fairbanks, and east to the town of North Pole and Eielson Air Force Base. It carries both passengers and freight, but ridership continues to decline.

The original intent of the Alaska Railroad was "to facilitate economic development and access to mineral deposits in the Territory of Alaska. Completed in 1923, the railroad was part of the Department of the Interior until the creation of the Department of Transportation, at which time the railroad became part of FRA. On January 5, 1985, pursuant to authority delegated by the Alaska Railroad Transfer Act of 1982 (45 U.S.C. 1201 et seq.), FRA sold the Federal Government's interest in the Alaska Railroad to the Alaska Railroad Corporation [ARRC], a public corporation of the State of Alaska. Today, the ARRC provides freight and passenger service from the ice-free ports of Whittier, Seward, and Anchorage to Fairbanks as well as Denali National Park and military installations. Vessel and rail barge connections are provided from Seattle, Washington and Prince Rupert, British Columbia." The federal government's interest was sold in 1985, yet federal taxpayers are still being railroaded to pay for its rehabilitation.

$1 Million for Park and Ride and a Passenger Shuttle System at the Alaska State Fair

According to the Alaska State Fair's official Web site, "The Fair has continued to grow. In 2001, more than 307,000 visitors attended the Fair. They saw, among other things, the more than 10,000 exhibits that the Fair now boasts. The Fair is also large enough to currently require 12 full-time employees, 420 temporary employees and 300 volunteers." Apparently, 2002 was a banner year for the State Fair, because a local Alaskan grew the largest cabbage ever at 105.6 pounds. But no one has weighed the cost of the federal subsidy (courtesy of Sen. Stevens)— about $3 per visitor, which could be added to the admission fee instead of being taken from the lower 48.

$400,000 for a Parking Lot and Pedestrian Safety Access in the Town of Talkeetna, Alaska

Joni Mitchell once sang, "They paved paradise and put up a parking lot." She certainly had no idea that the parking lot would cost $400,000 and be in a town of 800 people. Sen. Stevens could have instead just handed each resident a check for $500.

$4 Million for a Pedestrian Crossing on the Missouri River in Omaha, Nebraska

In 2001, Senate Appropriations Committee Member Robert Kerrey (D-Neb.) received a going-away present for his retirement. When he received the $4 million earmark, the retiring senator later acknowledged he probably "lost" $30 million in earmarks for the University of Nebraska alone. When he found out about his farewell gift, courtesy of his long-time buddy Sen. Richard Shelby (R-Ala.), Kerrey exclaimed, "Is this a great country, or what?"

$1 Million for the Savannah River Water Taxi

Looking for new and inventive ways to spend tax dollars, appropriators found that water taxis could be fun. This particular taxi will be used primarily to whisk tourists from Savannah to Hutchinson Island, thanks to House appropriator Jack Kingston (R-Ga.).

$260,000 for the Toonerville Trolley System

This trolley system hopes to preserve the memory of the early twentieth century comic strip of the same name created by Fontaine Fox. While the comic strip was very funny, the Toonerville Trolley System is not a barrel of laughs for taxpayers who don't live in Pelham, New York. The money will be used to purchase two "vintage-type" diesel-powered, handicapped-accessible trolleys.

$750,000 for Hovercraft Development in Toledo, Ohio

House appropriator Marcy Kaptur (D-Ohio) engineered $750,000 for this project. "Promotional" material sent out by the Ohio Lake Erie Commission in early 2001 noted that the next step for the hovercraft was for the potential private operator to determine the financial feasibility of this venture. In an October 2002 report, Brian Schwartz, the Toledo Lucas County Port Authority's communication director, said the craft, which would shuttle passengers between Toledo and Windsor, Ontario, would not be purchased until his agency renovates a marina into an entertainment district and builds a ferry terminal. The federal share of those projects has yet to be determined.

$1 Million for the Des Moines Riverwalk

This $1 million earmark in fiscal year 2004 will help fund a half-mile "swath of paths, bridges, and landscaping, hugging the banks of the Des Moines River." That means that Rep. Leonard Boswell (D-Iowa) will be back for seconds in 2005. According to a March 2004 *Des Moines Register* article, "Federal flood studies will indefinitely delay the Des Moines riverwalk project, which planners had hoped to complete in 2007. The U.S. Army Corps of Engineers says it needs at least an extra year to approve a design for the $26.4 million riverwalk, which was first pitched by Principal Financial Group in 2002. . . . They had hoped to celebrate completion in 2007. Now it looks as if major work on key components, such as a 'signature' pedestrian bridge, won't begin until then." The article went on to say that "meanwhile, at least two city leaders are irked that local taxpayers will foot more than $4 million of the riverwalk's total cost, a dramatic increase from the $880,000 estimate from only a year ago." Imagine how federal taxpayers feel about paying for this boondoggle.

$500,000 for Anaheim Resort Transit

Rep. Loretta Sanchez (D-Calif.) walked off with this earmark to fund buses in and around Disneyland. We're betting Sanchez won't need a Fast Pass to skip ahead.

Treasury/Postal: This Little Piggie Went to Court

The Treasury/Postal Service Appropriations Act is usually not contentious. One agency that it does fund is the General Services Administration (GSA). Known as the landlord of the federal government, GSA is responsible for the construction and maintenance of new federal buildings. In the early to mid-1990s, Congress had a fixation on building new courthouses. Not all of these new courthouses were needed, but that didn't stop Congress from believing that if you build it, they will come.

$25 Million for a Federal Building and U.S. Courthouse in Beckley, West Virginia

A 1990 GSA study found that Charlestown, West Virginia, was in greater need of a courthouse than Beckley. Both cities had requested a courthouse, but budget constraints only allowed one to be built. In 1990, $80 million was appropriated for a courthouse in Charleston. As a result of Beckley's patience, then–Senate Appropriations Committee Chairman Robert Byrd (D-W.Va.) saw to it that both a federal building and a courthouse were to be constructed in 1992, when both budget constraints and the deficit were greater—factors that did not impede Sen. Byrd's largess.

After the Beckley fiasco, the GAO reported in 1993 that U.S. courthouses were overstaffed and, in many districts, overbuilt, adding that "taxpayers risk overpaying by at least $1.1 billion in the next ten years for courthouses that the judiciary cannot justify because its methods for predicting its need for space are so badly flawed."

In 1994, the Senate Environment and Public Works Committee criticized the excessive cost of courthouse construction, stating "the majority staff found that substantial increases in Federal courthouse construction often have been accompanied by uncontrolled and excessive spending. The report recommended that "a moratorium be placed on the approval of all new federal courthouse construction until the construction program has been reformed."

Even with these two warnings, the following courthouses were funded in fiscal year 1995 (the first fiscal year after the release of the reports):

$23,200,000 for a courthouse in Long Island, New York
$6,446,000 for a courthouse in Corpus Christi, Texas
$5,640,000 for a courthouse in Albany, New York
$4,230,000 for a courthouse in Las Vegas, Nevada
$2,936,000 for a courthouse in Greenville, Tennessee
$2,914,000 for a courthouse in Covington, Kentucky

$120 Million for a Courthouse in Phoenix, Arizona

Mistaking the project for the Taj Mahal of justice, planners overestimated the building's size by 38,441 square feet, a decision that will mean an additional $1 million per year in maintenance costs. Then-Senate Treasury Appropriations Subcommittee Chairman Dennis Deconcini (D-Ariz.) pocketed this prize pork in 1994.

$2.8 Million for a Courthouse in Steubenville, Ohio

Congress continued with this project in 1995 despite criticism from local judges that an additional courthouse was unnecessary. In a letter to Congress, U.S. District Judge James Graham plainly stated, "In my opinion, the construction of a courthouse in Steubenville and the creation of additional judgeships there would be a monumental waste of the taxpayers' money."

$44.3 Million for Construction of the Albuquerque, New Mexico Courthouse

A May 1997 GAO report stated that the Albuquerque federal courthouse "is an example of how [the U.S.] can reduce the need for more courtrooms . . . in some districts."

GAO reported that the courtrooms in Albuquerque were used only 44 percent of total federal workdays in 1995, and on most non-trial days when the courtrooms were actually used, "courtrooms were used for two hours or less." Federal judges remarked that even with the newly built courthouse, they planned on sharing courtrooms more often than not due to constant travel. Yet, appropriators, particularly Sen. Pete Domenici (R-N.M.), felt it necessary to sink millions of dollars into the project. . . . $44 million for a courthouse to be used 44 percent of the time.

$2.4 Million for Design and Construction of a Federal Parking Facility in Burlington, Iowa

The $2.4 million earmark was added by the House to provide 200 parking spaces for 18 federal employees in Burlington, in the district of then–House Treasury/Postal Subcommittee Ranking Member Jim Lightfoot (R-Iowa). That's $12,000 per parking space and $133,333 per employee.

$22.6 Million for Courthouse Construction in Orlando, Florida

As part of the fiscal year 1997 Consolidated Appropriations Act, $9.5 million was added by the House for courthouse construction in Orlando, Florida. The earmark, which was inserted without a request from either the President or a chamber of Congress, was to be used to buy land adjacent to the current courthouse. In fiscal year 1999, appropriators spent an additional $1.9 million to begin construction of the structure in 2000. In 2002 and 2004, appropriators again gouged taxpayers for $4 million and $7.2 million, respectively, for the courthouse. Florida lawmakers were "ready to build" the $50 million, 157,600 square foot structure in 1994. That same year Rep. Bill McCollum (R-Fla.) claimed that then–House Speaker Tom Foley (D-Wash.) quashed the project to "punish" McCollum for giving money to Rep. Foley's opponent in the 1994 elections.

$6 Million for the U.S. Courthouse in Montgomery, Alabama

The $46 million facility was built to complement the famous Frank M. Johnson Federal Courthouse, site of landmark civil rights cases in the 1960s. Designers of the courthouse took special care to "closely match the original historic courthouse, built in 1932."

In 2002, Sen. Richard Shelby (R-Ala.) grabbed another $4 million for repairs and alterations to the Montgomery courthouse, just two years after construction of the structure was completed. Perhaps the architects should have taken better care to initially construct a reliable building instead of taking taxpayers to such an expensive court.

$3.5 Million to Build a New Annex of the Erie, Pennsylvania Courthouse

This project, which happened to be in the district of vulnerable freshman Philip S. English (R-Pa.), began in 1993. The original price of the new building was estimated at $20.5 million. But like most other government-funded projects, by 2001, the Erie courthouse cost estimates increased to more than $30 million.

$1.45 Million for the Pioneer Courthouse in Portland, Oregon

The historical Pioneer Courthouse was built in 1875 at the request of President Ulysses S. Grant and is home to the second oldest post office west of the Mississippi River. In its 2004 project report, the GSA pinpointed the building for seismic upgrades, causing an uproar. GSA's requests included installing driveway ramps and building an underground garage in the basement. Historical preservationists railed against the "destructive" construction of a historical site, and pointed out that GSA included the add-ons without authorization from Congress.

According to a 2003 statement from Rep. Earl Blumenhauer (D-Ore.), GSA was using security as an excuse to build the parking garage and ramps, but the alterations were really added to benefit the four U.S. Circuit Court of Appeals judges that reside there: "While it certainly may be more convenient for them to have parking in the building, using security needs as justification for the parking garage just doesn't make sense. Only one half block away is secure parking for these judges. Judges have been walking to this courthouse for more than a century, and according to federal Marshals, there has never been an incident. In fact, to install a driveway and parking garage will add an additional element of complexity to the security operation of the facility."

$152.6 Million for the Brooklyn, New York Courthouse

Chief Judge Charles Sifton was furious at the mismanagement of the Brooklyn courthouse construction, and wrote to the New York City Commissioner for Public Buildings, Robert Beck, that GSA, which oversees federal buildings, "is not competent to oversee the programme development, design, contract negotiation and construction of a large building project." Many feared that the $370 million building would be less adequate than the old courthouse it was replacing.

In fact, the situation was much worse than originally thought. The story behind construction on the Brooklyn courthouse is like something out of a mob movie. In October 1998, the U.S. Attorney's office in New York indicted six longtime employees of GSA and nine contractors in a kickback scheme involving numerous federal construction projects, including the courthouse.

Dating back to 1993, deals were made on construction of federal buildings in Brooklyn and Manhattan, with private contractors bribing GSA employees for steady work with gifts ranging from a few thousand dollars to $100,000 to vacation packages in Puerto Rico and Disney World. For sale were jobs like renovations to courtrooms, bathrooms, and offices in the Brooklyn courthouse. Some contractors were able to make back their bribe money by over-billing the government for services performed. The fiasco was revealed in 1996 when a contractor notified authorities that GSA thugs had given an employee a shakedown.

If that doesn't have taxpayers shaking their heads, Brooklyn U.S. Attorney Zachary Carter mentioned that "ironically, the federal building with the most widespread kickback-and-bribery abuses was the federal courthouse in Brooklyn, where the defendants will later be arraigned."

$84 Million for the Federal Courthouse in Denver, Colorado

Denver's Byron G. Rogers Federal Court Building received $83,959,000 in fiscal year 1999 for renovation of the "dowdy" courthouse. In a cost-saving effort, the House removed funding for the $84 million project, but Senate Treasury/Postal Appropriations Subcommittee Chairman Ben "Nighthorse" Campbell (R-Colo.) vowed that "it's in my bill, it's going to stay in my bill, and when we get to conference I'm going to put it back in. . . . It's a big project and I'm not going to let them strip it out of there." The senator blamed Reps. Diana DeGette (D-Colo.) and David E. Skaggs (D-Colo.) for not securing the project in the

House, but in the end, he was able to sneak $84 million back in during conference. Gloating over his victory, Sen. Campbell stated that "Colorado has every right to this money."

$35 Million for Food and Drug Administration (FDA) Consolidation

For years, the FDA has been requesting a consolidated campus. But one campus is supposed to be built in one Maryland county, and another campus is supposed to be built in yet another Maryland county, where a laboratory facility already exists. This is wasteful spending that benefits suburban counties in Maryland, not consolidation.

$300,000 for a Pilot Program That Will Assist Locally Owned Banking Institutions as They Bring Rural Communities into the New Economy

One of the goals of this program will be to increase Alaskans' exposure to the ATM (automated teller machine). Sen. Ted Stevens has plenty of experience with his own personal ATM, the Senate Appropriations Committee.

$640,000 for the Plains State Depopulation Symposium

Although the symposium will welcome representatives from several Midwestern states, it will be held at Dickinson State University in the state of Senate Treasury/Postal Appropriations Subcommittee Ranking Member Byron Dorgan (D-N.D.). Sen. Dorgan hopes these funds will find "public policies [that will] move more activities that used to be performed in big cities to rural areas."

Veterans Affairs/ Housing and Urban Development: Bacon Bits

Most people think that the committee structure in the federal government is confusing and in utter chaos. The Veterans Affairs/Housing and Urban Development Appropriations Act covers a myriad of programs ranging from VA hospitals, community development, the Environmental Protection Agency and NASA, confirming to American taxpayers that, at times, there is no rhyme or reason to the federal government's madness.

The Department of Housing and Urban Development is supposed to help the underprivileged. But in the mid-1990s appropriators found that helping themselves to taxpayer dollars is a lot more fun than helping the poor. Whether they are called Special Purpose Grants or the Economic Development Initiative Program, the programs that were initially set up to help the poor have been used to funnel pork-barrel projects into influential members' districts and states.

$1 Million for a Private Performing Arts Center in North Miami Beach, Florida

House appropriator William Lehman (D-Fla.) took this $1 million for a private performing arts center in North Miami Beach, Florida. The area is considered one of the more affluent areas in Miami. One has to wonder why taxpayers paid for something that would have been chump change for the people residing in their million dollar homes and sipping martinis poolside.

$2 Million for the Community Development Resource Center at Roberts Wesleyan College in New York

When Senate appropriator Alfonse D'Amato (R-N.Y.) grabbed $2 million for the Community Development Resource Center at Roberts Wesleyan College in Western Monroe County, one had to wonder if he planned on attending the widely respected business school. After all, D'Amato has had his share of scandals, from stock deals to ethics complaints. In fact, after a 19-month investigation into dozens of allegations in 1991, the Senate Ethics Committee criticized Sen. D'Amato for allegedly allowing his brother, Armand, to use his office stationery to contact Pentagon officials to help obtain defense contracts. D'Amato was chairman of the Banking Committee and also a member of the Defense Appropriations Subcommittee. His brother was subsequently convicted, but the conviction was later overturned; D'Amato got a heap of praise. Mike Donahue, spokesman for the Republican National Congressional Committee, put it this way: "It's very simple. Al D'Amato practices good politics—constituent service. There's nothing extraordinarily complex about it." That's one reason he was known as "Senator Pothole."

$150,000 to Develop the George C. Marshall Memorial Plaza in Uniontown, Pennsylvania

If there is a private non-profit organization named Friends of George C. Marshall, why do taxpayers have to foot a $150,000 bill to develop the George C. Marshall Memorial Plaza in Uniontown? It's because the friends of Marshall Plaza have a friend in Rep. John Murtha (D-Pa.).

$1.35 Million for Renovation of the Paramount Theater in Rutland, Vermont

VA/HUD Appropriations Subcommittee Member Patrick Leahy (D-Vt.) walked away with $1.35 million for renovation of Paramount Theater in Rutland, Vermont. He was lucky because this was the first year that President Clinton used the line-item veto, which some economists estimate could save taxpayers up to $5 billion a year. Sen. James Jeffords (I-Vt.) was hoping the theater would be spared. According to Jeffords, "The citizens of Rutland deserve the credit. They worked so hard to get this project started and to let the White House know how important it is to our downtown." It should be noted that Jeffords became one of four senators to file a lawsuit to repeal the line-item veto. "The line-item veto is a dangerous tool," he said. "I'm just glad that the Paramount Theater was spared." Never mind the rest of the country.

$2 Million for the Cleveland Avenue YMCA in Montgomery, Alabama to Build a Cultural Arts Center

Senate VA/HUD Appropriations Subcommittee Member Richard Shelby (R-Ala.) was responsible for this project. Few may argue with the YMCA's philosophy of putting "Christian principles into practice through programs that build healthy spirit, mind, and body for all." Nor is there much argument that they can offer physical fitness activities to the community, and more specifically to low-income people who cannot afford to pay for a membership in a private health club. But here's the problem: In recent years, some YMCAs have seemingly gone way beyond their tax-exempt mission to build start-of-the-art fitness centers that are now attracting an affluent clientele.

$3.22 Million to Enlarge and Update the Scarborough Library at Shepherd College in Shepherdstown, West Virginia

What would an appropriations year be without Sen. Robert Byrd (D-W.Va.)? Fairly quiet, probably. He reeled in $3.22 million to enlarge and update the Scarborough Library at Shepherd College in Shepherdstown, which boasts a whopping population of 803.

$1 Million for the Museum of Science and Industry in Chicago, Illinois, to Restore a German U-505 Submarine

When Sen. John McCain (R-Ariz.) criticized the approval of $1 million for the Museum of Science and Industry in Chicago, Illinois to restore a German U-505 submarine, one had to take notice because the senator had always stood up for veterans. The former decorated pilot called it a waste of taxpayers' money. The U-505 submarine was the only German submarine captured by the U.S. Navy during World War II and the code books seized from the submarine greatly assisted the Allied effort. In 1954, the Museum of Science and Industry took hold of the U-505. More than 24 million guests have visited the legendary vessel since then.

Today, the U-505 is a National Historic Landmark, the only U-boat of its type in the United States and the only Type IX-C

submarine left in the world. Because weather and pollution bat-
tered the U-505 while it was sitting outdoors, the idea now is to
move it indoors. Why they couldn't raise private money for this
restoration project had McCain up in arms. (Museums normally
charge a "suggested fee," although if you want to stand out and
have everyone snarl at you, you can claim poverty.) The submarine was closed to visitors in January 2004, but will return in the
spring of 2005 as part of a new 35,000-square-foot exhibit that
tells its story.

$350,000 for the Development of a Cultural and Community Center in Marin, California

Senate VA/HUD Appropriations Subcommittee Member Barbara Boxer (D-Calif.) convinced legislators to dump $350,000
into Marin, one of America's richest counties, and another
$500,000 into the city of Lancaster, evenly divided between re-
location of the 50th District Agricultural Association Fair-
grounds and construction of the $14 million National Soccer
Activity Center. The $250,000 gift was not enough to satisfy the
soccer crowd, and Boxer delivered another $740,000 in 2002
to finish the complex. At the same time, the Soccer Center continues to collect fees and accept $1,500 contributions. While
no one is against kicking the ball around, we just wonder why
California couldn't take a page from other states or private
youth clubs and use their fees to build their own fields.

$250,000 to Renovate and Revitalize the Westhampton Beach Performing Arts Center

Not to be outdone by Sen. Boxer and her desire to help out the wealthy in Marin, House appropriator Michael Forbes (R-N.Y.) decided to feed the rich in Westhampton Beach.

$4.5 Million for the University of Alaska Museum in Fairbanks

The university's museum has held such famous exhibits as Women of the Alaska Gold Rush, Not Just a Pretty Face— Evolution of a Doll Collection, and Fly Fishing and Book Making. It's a safe bet Sen. Ted Stevens was responsible for this money.

$300,000 for the Admiral Theater in Bremerton, Washington

House appropriator Norm Dicks (D-Wash.) walked home with $300,000 for the Admiral Theater in Bremerton, Washington. The community theater recently received a $4.2 million renovation and is considered the cornerstone of the revitalization efforts of downtown Bremerton. Dicks also secured $400,000 for this theater in the fiscal year 2000 Interior Appropriations Act. Talk about double dipping!

When Dicks was named "Porker of the Month" for using federal taxpayers' money to renovate a community theater, Dicks responded harshly: "These grants are for economic development that is totally appropriate under the legislation that created these laws," Dicks told the Bremerton *Washington Sun* newspaper. "The Admiral Theatre is crucially important to the revitalization of downtown Bremerton." According to the *Sun*, Dicks, a Bremerton native, said that in a Navy town, it's important to have facilities where sailors and officers can enjoy themselves. And, he said, the theater has been widely supported in the community, not only by local and state government agencies but by private citizens.

Nearly 60 percent of the $4.2 million raised to renovate the theater came from the private sector, but the federal government previously provided a $100,000 grant to put in an elevator system so the theater would comply with disabilities laws and a $1.5 million construction loan from 1996 that is just about to be paid off, he said.

Dicks also didn't appreciate being called a "porker." "I think it's totally ridiculous," he said. "These guys don't know what they're talking about. They never called my office. They're just trying to garner publicity. I wish they would be more responsible." Maybe if Rep. Dicks were more responsible with the taxpayers' money and followed proper budget procedure by submitting the grant to a competitive process, he wouldn't have earned such a (dis)honor.

$1.5 Million for the Construction of the $20 Million Stax Museum of American Soul Music in Memphis, Tennessee

When the Senate decided to give $1.5 million to the city of Memphis for the construction of the $20 million Stax Museum of American Soul Music, senators must have been in a funk. The museum is named after Stax records, one of the biggest studios for soul musicians from 1960 to 1975, and noted for winning an Oscar for the soundtrack to Isaac Hayes's *Shaft*. Its 500-seat auditorium is projected to improve local tourism and the Memphis economy. But it stands in stark contrast to the Jimi Hendrix Museum in Seattle, which was funded without a penny from the federal government.

$1 Million for the Gorilla Forest Exhibition in Louisville, Kentucky

House VA/HUD Appropriations Subcommittee Member Anne Northup (R-Ky.) managed to grab $1 million to help build the $15 million Gorilla Forest Exhibition in Louisville. Throughout the years, tens of millions of dollars from federal, state, and private funds have been dumped into the Louisville Zoo. But the latest influx of federal funds has more than just the gorillas pounding their chest. Officials are boasting about the revenues and record-breaking crowds visiting the exhibit. The average year's attendance is about 800,000, and most of them have come to see Frank, a 30-something Silverback, his two female companions, and five youngsters. Officials projected and predicted they would make mega bucks in this venture. Even if they borrowed the money, they knew they would be able to pay it back rather quickly. Instead, they got a permanent "loan" from taxpayers.

$930,000 for the Findlay Market in Cincinnati, Ohio

The Senate Appropriations Committee felt the need to squeeze $930,000 to help the Findlay Market expand in Cincinnati. The *Cincinnati Inquirer* put it this way: "Regular Findlay Market shoppers value the weekly ritual of squeezing through the market house aisle, surrounded by the smells of fresh fish and pork." That's certainly an apt description of the project.

$2.25 Million for Winter Recreation Opportunities in Alaska

Military and civilian persons at the North Star Borough Birch Hill recreation area in Alaska will get to live it up in the winter, thanks to their generous patron, Senate Appropriations Committee Chairman Ted Stevens (R-Alaska). It would be cheaper to buy all of them their own sled.

$2 Million for the St. Petersburg Sunken Gardens Improvement Project

House Appropriations Committee Chairman Bill Young (R-Fla.) sunk $2 million into this project. The Sunken Gardens used to be a huge tourist attraction. A developer representing some 50,000 nudists offered the city $2 million for the garden and planned to invest another $3 million to attract European nudists to the six-acre lot, but the city subsequently rejected the "Eden for nudists." Some feared the nudists might have gotten pecked by flamingos.

$250,000 to Fund the Culver City Theater Project

Senate appropriator Dianne Feinstein (D-Calif.) managed to walk off with $250,000 to fund the Culver City Theater project. Why it needed the cash is anyone's guess. Kirk Douglas and his wife Anna already dropped $2.5 million into the project. But why they even wanted this project may be a better question, because hundreds of citizens have protested the project. Here's what the "Citizens for a Livable Culver County" told officials at a public meeting: "Most residents react in disbelief when they learn that the Redevelopment Agency wants to put a large multiplex (up to 24 screens and 5,000 seats) right next to the school district office and Linwood E. Howe Elementary School. They wonder how the children playing in the playground will be affected by jackhammer construction noise, pollution that severely violates air quality standards, and increased traffic. They wonder whether moviegoers will really park up to three blocks away, rather than cruise streets near the cineplex to find free on-street parking. They wonder how police protection and fire safety will be affected, especially when one of the most severely impacted intersections is directly in front of the fire station."

$202,500 for Construction of the National Peanut Festival Agriculture Arena in Dothan, Alabama

House Appropriations VA/HUD Subcommittee Member Terry Everett (R-Ala.) may think it's peanuts for taxpayers, but $202,500 for construction of the National Peanut Festival Agriculture Arena in Dothan is still a hunk of change. After Sen. John McCain (R-Ariz.) criticized the arena funding during a speech on the Senate floor, Everett's press secretary, Mike Lewis, defended the appropriation. He took this swipe at McCain: "It's easier to point fingers and make jokes than to investigate how this money is being used. (McCain) likes to toot his own horn and promote himself more than anything."

"The National Peanut Festival is so much a part of the culture and the economy of the Wiregrass and the Tri-States, just as peanuts themselves," Everett gleefully declared upon getting the loot. "We've seen tremendous growth in the Festival's attendance in recent years, and this construction funding will help it keep pace with future growth and community need." What's more? We've learned they will even have a big parade!

$900,000 for the Denver Art Museum

According to its 2001–2002 annual report, the museum's foundation boasts assets with a market value of more than $35 million, yet Senate appropriator Ben "Nighthorse" Campbell (R-Colo.) felt it necessary to grab $900,000 to help fund the museum. Here's a question for you, senator: Did you flunk math, or what?

$90,000 to the American Film Institute in Los Angeles to Renovate the Facilities

By our calculation, that's two minutes of screen time for a well-paid actor. And they don't even have to be good actors.

The following NASA earmarks have shown taxpayers that pigs really can fly:

$7 Million Above the Budget Request for the Earth Observing System Data Information System (EOSDIS)

When NASA coined its new slogan—"faster, cheaper, better"—the agency certainly wasn't thinking of EOSDIS. NASA managed to get $7 million above the budget request for EOSDIS, which has been a controversial expenditure from the get-go.

EOSDIS collects integrated land, sea, and climatic data, covering everything under the sun. To put it in perspective, take a look at the 32-volume *Encyclopedia Britannica*, which contains more than 65,000 articles, or about 300M bytes of information. Imagine if EOSDIS averages two terabytes of data each day— that's comparable to nearly 7,000 *Encyclopedia Britannica* sets. That's a lot of data to interpret—and it will be simply impossible to interpret it all in any timely manner. The GAO criticized EOSDIS for its lack of cost-effectiveness and some scientists argue this research can be done for less than one-fifth the current cost. The debate raged on and appeared to come to a head in 1996 when then–House Science Committee Chairman Robert Walker (R-Pa.), who was critical of NASA's climate research programs, said he questioned whether the lifecycle costs, which the GAO estimated will cost $33 billion through 2020, would make EOSDIS unsustainable in future years.

$5 Million for the Consortium for International Earth Science Information Network (CIESIN) in Michigan

The Senate tacked on $5 million for CIESIN. It will become the ninth Distributed Active Archive Center for socioeconomic activities within the EOSDIS. Prior to 1993, CIESIN received more than $100 million in unauthorized funding.

The following Environmental Protection Agency earmarks would even make Mother Nature angry:

$400,000 to Handle the Maui Algal Bloom Crisis

Most people probably never heard of this "disaster" until Senate appropriator Daniel Inouye (D-Hawaii) convinced the Senate Appropriations Committee to hand him a check for $400,000 to handle the "Maui Algal bloom crisis." Researchers argue that harmful algal blooms (HABs) are one of the most scientifically complex and economically significant coastal issues facing the nation today, and claim virtually every coastal state has reported major blooms. Here's their argument:

🐷 Economic losses associated with HABs are conservatively estimated to exceed $1 billion over the next several decades;

🐷 HABs have direct and indirect impacts on fisheries resources, local coastal economies, as well as public health and perception; and

🐷 HAB toxins can cause human illness and death; halt the harvesting and sale of fish and shellfish; alter marine habitats; and adversely impact fish, endangered species, and other marine organisms.

While the scientists and researchers make the above three points, we admit we only have one major point to make:

🐷 In 1995, when the money was first appropriated, there was no "crisis" in Maui.

$900,000 for Environmental Restoration at Lake Walenpaupack

In 1926, the Pennsylvania Power Light Company built Lake Wallenpaupack and today it owns most of the lake's shoreline. But why isn't the company paying? House appropriator Joe McDade (R-Pa.) managed to grab $900,000 for environmental restoration at Lake Walenpaupack before retiring in 1998. It was a parting gift for his state. *The Pocono Record* had this to say of him: "To the end, McDade was a pork-barrel politician, and Monroe County was among his last beneficiaries. Thanks to McDade's clout, county government received a $3 million grant to build a new emergency communications center in Snydersville. . . . He came to the nation's attention in mid-1980s when news magazines profiled his political maneuvers to secure $66 million in federal aid to build the Steamtown Rail Museum in Scranton. Some called it an example of federal money being wasted. To business people in Scranton, it was a godsend that gave the aging city hope." He also is known as an indicted House member who was accused of taking $100,000 in vacations, gifts, and campaign contributions in exchange for helping defense contractors win contracts. But a local Pennsylvania jury acquitted him of criminal wrongdoing in 1996.

$1.3 Million to Assist in Job Retention for Agricultural Workers at the Hamakua Sugar Company in Hawaii

Remember the Archies' hit song "Sugar, Sugar"? We're betting Sen. Daniel Inouye (D-Hawaii) was singing it when he grabbed $1.3 million to assist in job retention for agricultural workers at the privately owned Hamakua Sugar Company in Hawaii. But like the song, the private company didn't stay on top very long. In March 1993, the company went bankrupt, leaving $38 million worth of unharvested sugarcane on 14,000 acres. A state government task force concluded that a harvest was possible but that a start-up state loan of $8 million was necessary. P. Ernest Bouvet, the former manager of the private company, was asked to do the final harvest, which he accomplished in 16 months. While they repaired the mill, which took two and half months, crews had difficulties working with broken equipment. The state finally interceded and shut down the mill with more than 500 acres of cane still standing.

What was the purpose of dishing out $1.3 million for a lost cause? We guess they were following one of Hawaii's ancient traditions—*holoholo wale*—which means to wander aimlessly, without a destination or purpose.

The preceding examples are just a sampling of Congress's excesses over the years, which have helped create a record $413 billion deficit and a $7.5 trillion national debt that will burden future generations. As Congress continues to spend more money, there will be thousands of silly and wasteful projects that will sneak their way into the appropriations bills. Be sure to visit Citizens Against Government Waste at *www.cagw.org* for continual updates on how your elected officials are squandering your money, and find out what you can do to stop the waste.

ACKNOWLEDGMENTS

This book was edited by Thomas A. Schatz, president, and David E. Williams, vice president, policy of Citizens Against Government Waste (CAGW). The material could not have been compiled without the help of the many research associates who have worked for CAGW throughout the years. Special thanks go to Angela French, the current research associate, and Tim Maier, Maryland city editor of the *Washington Examiner*.

INDEX